Success with International Customers

A Complete Guide for Real Estate Agents

Valeria Grunbaum

To Ray,

Much International Success

Valeria

Nov 2010

Success with International Customers

First published by Ecademy Press

Ecademy Press
6 Woodland Rise, Penryn,
Cornwall UK TR10 8QD
info@ecademy-press.com
www.ecademy-press.com

ISBN: 978-1-9058-2344-4

Printed and Bound by;
Lightning Source in the UK and USA

This book is printed on acid-free paper from managed forests. This book is printed on demand, so no copies will be remaindered or pulped.

Contents

Dedication

To my parents who with their example taught me about Real Estate. Thanks for your constant support and unconditional love. Thanks for teaching me that anything is possible if we act with passion toward it.

Acknowledgments

To Sadegh, my husband, for loving me the way you do and supporting me in all my crazy ideas. Thanks for challenging me and making me grow in the process.

To my brother, Pablo, and my sister, Carolina, thanks for loving me and for being always with me. I am very proud of you both.

To Cookie, my dog, for being my companion along the way of writing this book and bringing me joy during the stressful days.

To my best friend, Michele, thanks for being there for me and encouraging me to reach my dreams.

To my Grandma Mercedes, who passed away many years ago, for teaching me how to make my first sale when I was seven years old. Since then I knew I wanted to be in sales, and I know that you are having fun with me every time I am closing a sale.

To Ric for being a true friend every time I need it, and for showing me that everything is possible — I just have to ask for it.

To my mentor, Joe Williams, for inspiring me and showing me what could be possible. I will be grateful for life.

To Debbie Battersby for being a mentor and a friend in this process.

To Barbara, thanks for being my life coach, my professional coach and my friend.

To Noel, for being a mentor and a friend, and teaching me to have excellence in everything I do. Thanks for not accepting less than the best from me.

To Mindy and Jenny, for your guidance, support and encouragement during the process of writing this book. Without you both, it wouldn't be possible.

To Deborah Valledor for being a mentor and a role model. I will always be grateful for all that you have taught me and for your friendship.

To Teresa King Kinney, Letty, Maureen, and the staff at the Realtor® Association of Greater Miami and the Beaches for trusting in me and giving me the opportunity to teach and share what I know.

To Jeff Hornberger from the National Association of Realtors® and Ron Norton from the Florida Association of Realtors®, for your trust and support.

Thanks to the FT—you know who you are—my friends for life who teach me so much and hold me to my higher standards.

Thanks to all the sales agents who go to my conferences and trainings. Thanks to all of you who have reached out for coaching and expertise, because when I teach, I grow. And thanks to all customers, colleagues, professionals, co-workers, competitors, friends, etc., who have crossed my path in some way to teach me to be better in what I do and make me grow.

Introduction

Ever since I can remember, I have been watching my parents sell Real Estate. When I turned fifteen, I started working with them during my summer vacations. At that time, most of my parents' customers were international corporations looking for properties for their executives who were coming to work for the company for two to three years. That was my first experience in Real Estate and I loved it. When I decided to take a break from Real Estate and go to work in Corporate Sales at Intercontinental Hotels and later in Marketing at DHL, my passion for working with international customers increased. At the same time I discovered my desire and drive to teach and coach others.

In 1999 I started my own marketing consulting company in Venezuela. Three years later, an immigration lawyer and a Real Estate company in the US that specialized in international customers contacted my company. They hired us to develop their marketing in Venezuela. That is when I realized that I wanted to go back into Real Estate and develop my own International Real Estate business. I moved to Florida and got my Real Estate license. I soon as I started having success in my career, other agents approached me, and I now teach agents in the US and Venezuela how to work with international customers.

In the process, I have listened to many agents struggling with burn-out, or quitting after making small mistakes. They say that my little tips could have made the whole difference, so I decided that it is time to share what I've learned with anyone who wants to work in International Real Estate.

This book puts in the hands of Real Estate Agents information that has not been easily available in the past; namely, how to start working with international customers anywhere in the world. My intention is that this book becomes a guide that will help new and experienced Real Estate Agents get started and grow in the international arena. You may or may not agree with some of the techniques or the strategies. That is fine. My goal is not that you duplicate what I did, but that you find within these pages a few things you can adopt that will turn your business into an even more successful one than what I have.

In this book I talk about my own experiences working as an International Real Estate Agent in Venezuela and as a Realtor® in the USA*, and I share what has made me successful with international customers in both countries. Though my examples are with English- and Spanish-speaking countries, this book is written for International Real Estate Agents around the globe. Each country has its own laws and regulations about how to practice Real Estate, so make sure that your International Real Estate business is based on what is legal in your country and your target market. If you are not sure, please consult with your local board or association.

Valeria Grunbaum

www.ResourcesForInternationalRealEstateAgents.com

* Realtors® are Real Estate Agents who are members of the National Association of Realtors®.

CHAPTER 1
WHY WORK WITH INTERNATIONAL CUSTOMERS

Facts

Today's Communication:

In today's world, doing business worldwide becomes easier. The Internet gives us access to almost every corner of the globe in just seconds. It's an era where we can reach almost any customer, and where we compete to the highest level with thousands if not millions of people who have access to the same tools and information. But guess what? Most of the people DO NOT use what is available to excel in international business.

Having a website is the best way to show what you have to offer and give added value to your customers, so if you are thinking to go international or you are already there, a website is a MUST-have. Now we have the ability to build our own website in just a few hours, and maybe minutes if you buy one of those ready-to-go websites, and the price is just a fraction of what it used to cost. In 1999, my first website cost about $4,000 and took about 30 days of development; today I recommend going for the easiest way, and for less than $1,000 you can get a professional Real Estate website up and running with all the content and tools that you may need. It comes with user-friendly software to do your own updates so you do not have to pay extra for changes on your website.

1

You'll need to take care of many things after you build a website, and the most important one is marketing. This is critical, and if you do not promote your site no one will go there. In later chapters I talk more about marketing and promoting yourself.

The Internet has tools to help you promote your name and to connect and network with others, like Facebook, LinkedIn, MySpace, Google videos, YouTube, Ning, etc. Some are more professional than others, but all of them offer a way to get you out there and be part of the "Viral Loop" of social networks. Basically you have access to the friends of your friends' friends. When you get your name out there you are promoting yourself, and you can use social networking to promote and/or support your business. My recommendation is that you take your time to ask why you want to use these services and how each one is going to help your business and your customers. Whatever tools you choose, just make sure that you use them professionally, because I have seen lots of Real Estate Agents who scare customers instead of attracting them. These places are to connect with people, so decide how you want to use each social network. Be considerate in the way that you use each one. You may be in each social network for different reasons. For example, you could be in Facebook for hobbies and fun, and use LinkedIn for your business.

Email has a huge advantage over regular mail: You can reach more people in less time; you can get an instant receipt when they read it; and instead of days or weeks to receive a response, it usually comes almost immediately. I recommend having an email address that is related to your business and that is not from a free email service. For example yourname@yahoo.com could work perfectly as a personal account but does not look professional, so I believe that is a must to have an email account that shows that you own a business: yourname@yourbusiness.com.

What I see most common is that Real Estate agents use the email account that the Broker gave them, and guess what?! That is the Broker's email, not yours, so if you leave the company for some reason, or the company closes, you lose all the business that you could be receiving from marketing activities that you did in the past, business cards that you distributed, etc. Be smart on this one and buy a domain name with your name; i.e., if you are a sales agent and you work for a Broker company, get your own email address.

Make sure that the email service provider you are using allows you to see the emails from any server (most of them do). This is very important because you want to make sure that you have access to your emails from anywhere in the world, from any type of computer and Internet access. Some countries do not have reliable Internet services like we do in the US; some countries still work on dial-up, and broadband is still a luxury that some cannot access yet.

Making calls internationally is becoming easier every day. I am afraid to talk about this technology here because I know that while I am writing there are new things coming out, and by the time you read this book the information may be out of date. Let me just say that there are different ways to connect with customers in real time, either with text or voice. I always ask my customers where they have their IM (instant messaging) account, and I make sure to open an account there to have instant contact when they need me. Personally I use Skype most often, and I found out that most of my customers do too, but there are other services with similar features, like hotmail and yahoo. If you prefer to call phone-to-phone, you can also use the Internet with a service like VoipStunt or Skype. And I highly recommend searching for calling cards. If you are in the US you will find that several companies offer calling cards. Different per-minute rates apply, depending on where you want to call, but in most cases the cost is affordable. My recommendation is that if you are going for the calling card, shop around. I know that sounds weird shopping around for a calling card, but if you are going to call like I do internationally, finding the right calling card will save lots of money. Also you may want to check if the country that you target has a local phone number that can be forwarded to your phone in the US. That is a great service for your customers so they won't have to pay for an international call to reach you, and they think that you are more available for them. The cost to you is usually a flat rate between $30 and $50, but again that can change with all the new companies coming on the market. Just make sure that you make the right choice because once you have your number you do not want to change it. Don't make the same mistake that I did when I started doing business in the US: I signed a contract with a company that was selling local lines in Venezuela, so I got mine and I did all my marketing material plus an email campaign, business cards, etc. Then this company disappeared for a while. I lost my connection and a few months later one of my customers told me that he called me on that number and somebody else responded. The irony was that this "somebody" was a mortgage broker! I guess that she was getting some of my customers with free advertising.

For my fax service I use eFax, but I know that other companies offer electronic fax service, some for free and some for a small fee. Just make sure that you can receive faxes on your email so you can have them and read them in any part of the world.

Today's communications makes it easier to do business. Take full advantage of what this technology offers to international professionals.

Market Conditions:

International investors have their eyes on the US Real Estate market for different reasons, so it's important for you as a professional to understand where the strengths of the US Real Estate market are as compared to the weaknesses of an international investor's local market. Then you can offer a real reason to invest in the US instead of their local market or even in a different country.

Market conditions are in constant flux so make sure to be updated, not only on your local market, also on what's going on in the market(s) that you are targeting.

The US Real Estate Market in the Last Fifty Years:

The RE market in the last fifty years has been a cyclical market — you have a few years going up, then a few years of correction and stabilization, but at the end of the day the tendency of the market is to go up.

One of the biggest reasons we are expecting an increase in housing prices in certain areas is because the baby boomers are moving to retirement areas, or buying second homes, or investments.

Also, with the dollar going down against the Euro, European investors are looking to buy Real Estate in the US.

Immigration is also important to keep your eye on. Depending on the area where you are located, you will have people moving from different countries. In South Florida we have an increase of buyers from South America, either because they are moving to the US or buying properties as investments because they believe that their money is safer in the US compared to countries where there is political instability.

I don't want to give you data in this book because this book is to give you tools and tips to develop your international business no matter if the market is going up or down, but data is important. Make sure to do your research about your specific area and your potential customers so you have the information you need to make smart decisions on your action plan. If you go to the store at www.Realtor.org, you will find several reports with lots of current data and facts.

Why Invest in the USA:

International investors are looking for stability, security, and a safe place where they can invest their money.

One of my customers asked, "Why should I still invest in Real Estate in the US when the market is going down?" My response was that as a Real Estate investor you can make money when the market is going up or when the market is going down. What matters is the particular property that you are buying or selling, and what matters the most is that the numbers make sense in that particular investment. Real Estate investors are making money right now, and if you read the stories about the biggest millionaires in the US you will find out that millionaires have also been created when the market is going down. I do not perceive the market going down as a bad thing, because you can make money in ups or downs. It's the strategy that matters the most.

Diversifying

Seasonal Clientele:

What I've found out over the years is that a lot of the Real Estate investors buy properties in the US when they are visiting the country, so knowing when they are coming is critical to your business. Each country has different dates when a large number of visitors is expected. For example, Venezuela has the school summer vacations between July and September, while Argentina has theirs between December and February, so we see more visitors from those countries during those specific months. If you are planning to work with more than one country, I strongly recommend having a calendar where you've marked all the vacation dates so you can prepare your advertising and promotions around them. You will be able to plan a strategy that responds to the different seasons.

In addition to seasonal happenings, you also need to know what's going on in the country you're targeting. To give you an example, if one country is having political problems and that creates insecurity and instability, you may see an increase of customers from that country with the intention of bringing their money here and investing it where they believe it's going to be safe. You have to be aware of what's going on in the different markets and identify opportunities that will bring you business. I have seen spikes in my sales when something is going on in one of the countries that I am targeting, and the season could last months or years, depending on what is happening. I remember a few years ago lots of people from Colombia were investing in Real Estate in the US because of the political situation there. As soon as things in Colombia started to get better, the Colombian Real Estate market started going better also, and the people who invested here began moving their money back to Colombia to invest. I saw the same thing happen with Argentinean investors.

Preparing for Ups and Downs:

Because the market is cyclical/seasonal in many ways, you have to be prepared for the ups and downs and find your niche for each opportunity. The way to beat the cycles is go with the flow, be flexible enough to work with buyers and sellers, and dance with the seasons. What I mean by that is simple: There are seasons that people will buy so you work with buyers; there are seasons where people are selling so you work with sellers.

There are different types of investments within the Real Estate arena. We had a huge wave of customers buying pre-construction condominiums all over the US; now you see more people looking for properties that are in default and cannot close, or properties that are in foreclosure. If you are aware of what is going on the market and you really want to be ahead of your competition, I recommend that you to invest the time to understand how each of these different opportunities works so you can offer your customers what fits best for them.

Just remember that Real Estate is an active market. Again, it does not matter if the market is going up or down, there are always people buying and/or selling. Are you willing to do what it takes to be flexible enough that you can have the ability to work with customers in any market situation? If your answer is NO, then I say that you may also become a cyclical Real Estate Agent.

Why Diversify:

I know that lots of people will disagree with this one, because I found out that most of the Real Estate Agents like to specialize in one type of product, but being flexible and open to adapting my business to the needs of my customers, instead of trying to pull my customers into what I am working on, has been critical to my success. Customers usually know what they want, and if they do not think that you understand what they are looking for, they will find somebody else to work with.

Ever since I was young I was told to "do what successful people do." You'll notice that the biggest corporations diversify their products, and successful business people diversify theirs. So why not to use the same strategies that the successful companies and business people do?

When the market changes, you have to adapt to the market. If you are one of those people who has being doing the same thing for years and your results have changed, try getting out of your comfort zone and see what happens. Try new techniques, reach new markets, offer new products, and be flexible enough to play the game to the highest level.

One of the benefits of diversifying your business is that you are also diversifying your risk. For example. if there is a change in the market from Residential to Commercial, you are ready to provide for your customers. Remember that as the market changes, people will be migrating from one type of RE investment to another. You can also diversify by targeting different countries – if the market changes in Colombia and investors are not interested in buying in the USA anymore, you will have people from Mexico investing in RE in the US. By being flexible, you have a safety net and your income won't be as affected as when your whole business depends of one country. You can also diversify your type of customer. I have a well balanced portfolio of international customers, in which I have investors, second-home buyers, buyers that are relocating, and sellers. If you have a portfolio of customers that is balanced, you have less risk of being caught in a slow market.

One of the things that I would like to make VERY clear about diversifying is that you have to do it with a plan, because diversifying needs a strategy and doing it without a plan can cost your business lots of money.

The World Is Your Marketplace:

I encourage you to see the world as your marketplace. Right now you have almost-immediate access to any country in the world, and you can truly develop your business and be successful because there are unlimited opportunities in today's marketplace.

Opportunities and challenges will come to you, and it is your choice to say Yes or No. In my case I do not say No to any request that my customer asks me to do. If it is something that I do not know how to work with because it is not my area of knowledge, I find the right people to do it and team up with them to give the result that my customer wants.

It is funny how other Sales Agents look at me when they ask me where my "farm" area is. I always respond, "The world! I specialize in the International Customer," and most of the time they don't get it. I'm not saying that what I do is right or wrong, but it is what works for me, and it is the way that I found myself being more productive.

Understanding the International Market

Basic Differences between Local and International Customers:

I would like to go over some basic differences I have found between Local and International customers.

I work a lot with Latin American customers. The most common reasons they buy Real Estate in the US are that they think their money is safer here, they have more return for their investment, they have access to mortgages so they can leverage their money, they feel secure about their personal property ownership, they want to diversify their risk in different countries, they are looking for their second home in their preferred vacation place, or they are immigrating/relocating, etc. Underneath it all, they are looking for security and more certainty.

The international customer likes to shop around with different Real Estate Agents because in most of the countries there is no MLS system where Agents have access to all the properties that are for sale. In most of the countries each Real Estate Agent has their own listings. I had a customer from Latin America who, after seeing a property with me, called another Real Estate Agent and asked him for a better price for the same property. I lost the customer because the Developer agreed to give him a discount on the price and reduce the Agent's commission! I have to say that was smart of the other Agent and very inappropriate for the Developer, knowing that this customer was registered already as our customer with them. I ended up losing the customer and about $50,000 in commissions… and it still hurts. BUT I learned my lesson, and I explain how to protect yourself from this type of situation in the following chapters.

I have found that most of my International customers do not understand the Buyer / Agent concept, so is important to explain that to them. Also, the "value add" that they will have when working with an Agent that is representing them. I strongly recommend taking the ABR® (Accredited Buyer Representative) designation course, as it will give you more knowledge if you want to be specialized on the Buyer's side.

When an International Customer wants to sell a property, explain what the "exclusive right of sale agreement" means, because most countries do not use exclusive agreements, and sellers give the property to several agents to find a buyer.

The most critical part is that the majority of countries don't require that a person who wants to work in Real Estate have a Real Estate License. Anyone can sell Real Property and make a commission, and that has made this career of working with customers from other countries challenging. In my early years doing Real Estate in Venezuela, I worked with my parents at their Real Estate office. One of my first shocking experiences in this business was when I went with my first buyer to show a property, and there was a lady waiting for us in pajamas and flip-flops. She introduced herself as the Real Estate Agent for the property! Most countries have no requirements about education or preparation in the law and ethics, so one of the challenges I have found in the last few years is seeing sales agents in those countries selling properties in the US without a license. My recommendation is to educate your customers! I always carry the NAR®information that says that selling Real Estate in the US without a license is illegal, and I make sure to talk about that with the customer and explain why it is so important to work with someone who has a license in the state where the customer is looking to buy. I also try to educate every Real Estate Agent that I meet in the countries I have being working with, and I explain why it is so important to work with a US Real Estate Agent instead of selling directly.

Establish a System:

Each country has a different way to do business. You need to establish a system that allows you to keep control and helps you to follow up with your customer.

– Keep everything in writing

Keep everything in writing, especially when you talk in person or over the phone. After you finish your conversation, send an email with a summary of what you have talked about and agreed to. This is very important, as you want to avoid any misunderstanding due to the differences of language. And even though you both speak the same language you may be using terminology that the customer did not understand or misunderstood. By having everything in writing, you confirm what agreements were made, and the customer has an opportunity to review the conversation and ask questions. You need to be very clear in and keep written records of every part of the process. Remember, most of your customers are not used to doing business in the US, which is totally different from what customers are used to in their countries.

– Keep your oral and written communication formal

A week ago I went with a customer to see a condo. The agent at the sales office was trying to be nice and friendly and make a couple of jokes. My customer was totally distracted, thinking that he was hitting on her. By the time we finished the presentation she was so upset and offended that she did not want to do anything with that sales agent. Not all countries communicate the same way, and an innocent mistake like being more friendly than a customer is used to in their country could cost you the customer or, even worse, can be misunderstood and get you in trouble. This is where I see a lot of sales agents fail: Little things become the turn-off for the customer. I will go over more details about cultural differences in following chapters.

– Encourage the customer to get a lawyer during the process of doing business in the US

As sales agents we cannot give legal advice BUT we have to let the customer know how important it is to have legal advice during their Real Estate buying and selling process. Each country has laws and processes different from the US's, and it is very important that the customer gets in contact with a Real Estate lawyer specializing in international customers, to explain all the legal aspects of the process. All the contracts in the US are in English and most of the international customers do not speak the language well enough to understand some of the legal terms. Even some native speakers of English don't understand contract terms! At the same time, there are rules here that do not apply in their countries. I know that there are translations of some of the contracts and that's fine, but as a professional you need to make sure that your customer is totally aware of every legal aspect and is protected by a professional in the legal field.

Control

Taxes:

I always heard that in the US only two things are certain: Death and Taxes. I know that sounds funny, but that gives you a clear message of how important it is to pay taxes in this country. There are lots of countries where the governments are lax about taxes, or they call property taxes by a different name; for example, *Rates*. I encourage you to explain to your customers how important it is to pay property taxes here. I can tell you that every time I say to my customers that if they do not pay the taxes they will lose the property, they always make the same face. They cannot believe that can happen. It is very important that you explain how they must take this seriously. At the same time you have to encourage them to talk to an accountant specializing in Real Estate and international customers. It is very important that the accountant specializes in international customers, as some countries have an agreement with the US so the citizens do not pay taxes in both countries. You also want to make sure that your customer understands the different commitments that they have for doing business in the US. One thing I recommend always to my customers is to ask the bank to include the property taxes in the monthly mortgage payment.

Mortgages:

I like to ask my customers how the banks and mortgage system work in their country, so I can address the differences. The first question that you may want to ask your customer is if they have had a mortgage before. You will find that 50% of them, maybe more, never had a mortgage before. Give them all the information they need, no matter how basic it seems to you.

I always recommend that they leave two or three months' estimated monthly payments in an account and allow the bank to get the money directly from that account, if for some reason they cannot send the money on time.

Condo/Homeowners Association and Other Maintenance Payments:

Again it's just a matter of explaining how important it is to pay on time, and what the consequences could be of not doing so. I always like to suggest that my customers have a bank account where they can put the money for the association dues and other fees and ask the association to debit directly from the account. It's less headache for my customer and for the association. Just keep in mind that if the association /administration company changes, your customer will have to send the approval to the bank again. I recommend that my customers review the account every month to make sure they are being charged, and the moment that does not happen they need to follow up with the association immediately.

Rental Payments:

A lot of my customers buy properties and then we find a tenant for them. A couple of years ago a customer from Latin America to whom I'd sold a condo called me, complaining because the tenant had not paid the rent since moving in six months prior. So I referred him to a lawyer immediately to take care of the eviction process, which took about a couple of months. If he had told me the first month that the tenant was late, maybe the outcome could be different. And even if eviction was the result, he wouldn't have lost almost a year of rent.

When I asked him why he did not contact me or a lawyer sooner, he said that he "trusted the tenant because in US people respect the law...." What I want to show you with this example is how the perception that this customer had about doing business in the US cost him money and time.

By the way, I have to say that this customer was impressed by how fast the lawyers were able to evict the tenant. Where he came from, if you have a tenant who does not pay the rent, it could take years to get him out, plus a lot of lawyer expenses. So believe it or not, in spite of the bad experience with the tenant, this customer felt more confident in continuing to invest in Real Estate in the US because he believes our legal system will protect him as the landlord in these situations.

Opportunities

What I love the most in my career working with international customers is the opportunity to teach, to really make a difference. If they chose to shop around for other sales agents, I always tell them up front something like, "If you are talking with other Real Estate professionals, I encourage you to ask the following questions so you will know how much they know and who is the right person to work with you." Ninety percent of the time they come back to me. The reason is because only a few of us take the time and effort to learn and train in this arena.

Most of the customers that you will work with have no or maybe a little experience with the US Real Estate market, so you have the opportunity to become their resource. If you support them before, during and after, I can assure you that you will be ahead of the competition.

Laws and Government Regulations

Immigration: ASK AN EXPERT!

I remember listening in a seminar to a well known immigration lawyer about many investors who had bought properties as their way to get an investors visa, and then when they applied most of them were not approved. He made the comment that some Real Estate Agents are using the argument to sell real estate to foreign customers who want to move to the US. Be careful with this one; remember, we are not allowed to give any legal advice. The customer trusts us, so the best way to deal with this is to refer the customer to an immigration lawyer and make sure that they get their questions answered before you sell them a property for the wrong reasons.

The INS has different types of visas people can qualify for, depending on various factors. You should not under any circumstances give legal advice, but you can have a list of names and phone numbers of immigration lawyers whom you trust and whom you can refer your customers to. Once they are clear about the law, then it is time to help them find the right property.

Maybe you have a customer who is looking for a property for living purposes while they are going through the immigration process. I always make sure that they are already working with a lawyer.

This is a hot topic because at the end of the day you do not want to have a customer who invests all his savings in a property that he expects to live in or use for immigration purposes, and then, if the visa is not approved, must sell the property in distress because he needs the money to go somewhere else.

I strongly recommend having a personal, educational meeting with a lawyer to ask them about the types of visas and how the immigration process works so you can understand the risks and also the chances that foreign customers take when they are planning to move to the US. Ask your local Board of Realtors®. Sometimes they invite immigration lawyers to give a seminar to the Realtor®.

Federal Taxes:

There are huge differences in the way that countries manage their tax policies, so you want to make sure that your customers have the advice of a tax expert in the US and in their country. I also encourage you to have a conversation with an accountant knowledgeable about the country you are working on so you get the whole picture. Even though you cannot give advice, understanding how it works will make you a better and more efficient professional.

State Taxes:

OK, this is a huge one. Did you know that a foreign national will be taxed on their investments in the US if they die? This is another reason why the customer needs a lawyer to help the customer create the best business structure for their investment goals.

Legal Structures:

There are several ways of buying properties in the US, and international customers qualify for some of them. In order for them to choose which is the best one for them, the lawyer will go over several questions so they understand the whole picture, and will give them advice about the best option. A mistake in this area can cost the customer lots of money, so advise them to get this clear with an attorney before they close the property. And one more thing: Lawyers and accountants are the best ones to do the company registration, even though there are people who like to do it by themselves on the Internet; for example, on http://www.sunbiz.org.

The Buying and Selling Process:

Usually customers make appointments in advance, but it also could happen that it is Sunday morning and you are having breakfast and someone calls from a hotel, saying, "I am in town and I want to know if you can show me some properties today." The main thing that I want to do first, especially if I do not know how they do business in their country and I didn't have time ahead to prepare, is to ask questions to understand differences. I speak to the differences so they know what to expect. You need to have a list of questions that you can take with you to help you understand your customers in the first ten minutes of the conversation.

If I don't know much about the country this customer is from and I have enough time to prepare, I contact a local Real Estate Agent familiar with that country and ask for help. Usually they agree, and most of the time it is a great opportunity to establish a new business relationship with a local professional. Then I go over the questions with the local agent, so when I meet with the customer I am fully prepared to explain the process, making emphasis on the differences, so they are clear on what is going to happen and how it is going to work. I always like to address the differences like this: "I understand

that in Your Country usually this part of the process happens in this way.....
Here in the US instead it will be in this way..... " In these sentences you are
confirming the information you already have and are making clear that there
is a difference.

The main challenge that I have found during the years is that some customers
are uncomfortable to sign the contracts in English if they do not speak English,
so if possible I get them a copy in their language so they can read it. But again,
I explain why it is so important to have a lawyer who supports them on the
legal part of the process.

Some customers do not want to travel for the closings, and there is a way to
close a property at the US Embassy in their country. It is an easy process and
will make a huge difference in the deal if traveling could be an issue for the
customer. We have a customer from Argentina who is a doctor, and one of his
complaints about investing in the US is that it is far and he does not want to
deal with traveling back and forth. For him it is very convenient to close his
properties at the US Embassy in Argentina.

CHAPTER 2
HOW TO START

You can do business with international customers in several ways, but if you want to do it professionally, for long-term and get the best results in terms of time and money invested, I recommend the following steps that will make you stand out in the market.

First, Learn the Basics

Facts:

Know the numbers on how the market is acting. Go back at least three years and compare year by year, and sometimes month by month, if you want to work with different markets and you want to identify the peak seasons.

Once you choose the countries you want to target, start researching. Find out the history of that country, what is going on there now that is making investors bring their money to the US. If it's a political situation, find out how that can affect the investment of your customers. Also find out if what is happening is just a seasonal situation or if they do invest in the US as part of their culture.

You also want to understand where they are buying. Don't invest time and money to develop a target market if there's no interest to buy in your local market. Also, identify what types of properties they are buying. For example, from 2002 to 2006 a huge wave of investors from Latin America bought condos on pre-constructions projects in the South Florida area and Las Vegas, so all the marketing efforts went to promote those products. As the business climate changed, the marketing and the interest of the customers changed. Do your homework so you'll be more efficient when you work on your marketing plan.

Find out how your potential buyers are buying. By that I mean, do they use local Real Estate Agents to refer them to US Real Estate Agents? Do they research online? Do they look for Agents who do not have any type of connection with their countries, or ones who have lots of connections? These little details will tell you a lot and help you to decide which country you want to focus on first.

Techniques:

Rather than reinvent the wheel, find out the techniques they use locally that have been successful. In other words, how do they promote in their own market? What do they do to sell their own Real Estate? What gives them success?

Research their business culture. You want to know how they do business because you want to honor and respect their ways.

Prepare Yourself

Research:

If you are a US native or from a country other than the one that you want to target, you must take the time to review some words that may have different meanings than you know. Avoid using slang, and it will be smart to learn the lingo for the Real Estate process there, so when you are talking with them about the process in the US you will be able to talk in their own vocabulary.

I wish someone had told me this before I went to my first international business meeting in Colombia. For about thirty minutes I was talking with a coworker from Colombia, and at one point she stopped me and started laughing. She said that I should not use that word in Colombia because is a bad word and totally changed the meaning of the sentence! I learned my lesson and now, before I go to a new country I do my research and I feel more confident.

In my first trip representing a major hotel chain, I was being introduced to a female executive. When I was about to shake her hand she took my arm and basically shook it. That is the way women in that country shake "hands."

Learn about the local business etiquette because you want to be aligned with them so they are comfortable doing business with you. Business etiquette includes the way they shake hands, or dress, or even their protocol about conducting business meetings. When I was working for the hotel chain they were constantly training us about this. It's amazing how those little differences can either make the customer feel disrespected or totally honored.

Learning about their holidays can be useful because some countries celebrate different festivities than ours, as well as some of the same ones but on different dates, like Mother's Day. If you decide to create a marketing program around recognizing your customers on those special days, make sure you are contacting them on the correct day.

When I am traveling, I love to talk to the taxi drivers, the waitresses and people who work at the hotels because it's an easy way to find out about the country's values, what is important for them, as well what is going on, and what the political and economic situation is overall. That will give you an insight about things that you may not find in books, trainings, or websites. Talking with local people, observing the surroundings, going to a local supermarket will give you tons of information that will help you to even better understand the culture.

Economics:

Understand how the currency exchange works in the country you've targeted. To give you an example, countries like Venezuela are not under a Currency Exchange control, and the banks are not allowed to change more than X amount of dollars per year. In some countries they may be able to exchange money, but because there is a high demand for dollars, the exchange rate could be very high and going up. Why is this important to know? Because you want to make sure that your customer is able to pay the mortgage, taxes, condo association fees, etc. Most of my customers come from Venezuela, and even though there is a very strong exchange control there, most of them already have money in the US because there has been a culture of taking one's savings out of the country for as long as since I can remember.

About three years ago I wanted to expand my portfolio into new countries. When I did my research, I realized that two of the countries I wanted to work with did not have investment potential in Real Estate in the US. In the first case, it was because most of the people in that country did not make enough money to buy in the US, and the only ones who could make it were from the upper class, which was a small group. Besides, most of them were already known for investing lots of money in their own country. Any effort in time and money on my part would have been huge compared to the return on investment that I might expect, so I am glad I did the research before I started investing in marketing in that country.

Politics:

Some countries have agreements with the US. You want to know if there is such an agreement and how it can affect customers in their buying or selling process. It is also useful to know about the international agreements because that could give you the opportunity to develop a niche there that goes along with what the agreement says.

Some countries have strong laws about exporting money or about currency exchange control. Make sure that you understand it and talk to your customer to make sure that he will be able to make the payments.

Taxes are one of the things that can affect the foreign national, so make sure that the accountants they choose understand the tax law in that country.

Target Market

Once you define the niche market you want to focus on, learn from them so you will be aligned and your business relationship will be successful. That will turn into closings and referrals.

Who Is Your Customer?

This looks like a very basic question, but if you take the tiniest details seriously you will have easier and more efficient communication with the customer. While I was in Corporate sales at the hotel chain, my work consisted of getting more companies to use the facility for their guests and their events. In my process of visiting the companies, I began to understand how important it was for me to know with whom I was meeting that day. I could tailor-make a message for them. To give you an example, if I was about to meet with the CFO I would focus on pricing, discounts, and benefits in terms of money they would save by doing business with us. If my meeting was with the Marketing Manager, I talked about how our hotel was one of the landmarks of the city and how staying there would motivate the sales people. If the meeting was with the Human Resources department, my speech was totally different. Because I thought about what was the most important thing for them to evaluate for the company, I became successful when closing the sale.

Another key thing to help you know your customers is to identify their roles in the decision-making process. I have customers who make the decision as a couple, but in some cases you have the decision-maker and the influencer, and you want to make sure that your message gets to both if you want to close the deal. Three years ago I got a customer who was looking for investments, so I presented different properties. When he decided, I went to his home so he and his wife could sign the contract. At their house they started a disagreement because the wife thought he was losing his head doing Real Estate, and she was upset with him. Here I am in the middle of a discussion between husband and wife about whether to sign the contract, and after about two hours of answering the wife's various questions, to the point that I was feeling totally out of place, I decided they were not ready to buy as a couple. I stood up and said that I was leaving and to call me when they thought they were ready to do this together. While I was walking to the door the wife said that it was OK and they signed the contract.

After seeing the way that they behaved with each other in a couple of more deals, I realized that they were having a fight for power in the relationship and that it has being reflected in anything that they did together. Now when I have a meeting with them I know that I will have two conversations at the same table at the same time. In other words, the same message, different focus.

Once you know your target customer, you want to know the best strategies to use with them, and I will be talking in detail later in this book to help you apply some techniques and tools.

Tools for Marketing:

Each country or city has different ways to communicate with their community, and you will need to learn from each the specific marketing tools that work best to get to the market you are focusing on. If you are working with different countries at the same time, you will be amazed to see how the same things give different results in different countries. What makes you successful in one country may not in another. I like to separate the Marketing resources in two when I do my marketing plan:

Mass Media—any type of media that goes to the masses, like TV, radio, magazines, billboards and newspapers.

Direct Media—where the target is more specific; for example, events, emailing or mailing campaigns, direct promotions.

Find out what media are available for you in the target market and check out numbers, like the percent who respond and the rate of closing (if that information is available). Some media experts have general numbers so you can determine whether it would be worth it to invest. When you ask for the analysis of the media, it is important to have already defined your target audience so they can give you more realistic numbers. Once you have the comparison of the different media, decide what will be more profitable for you and prepare the information for your marketing plan.

Study the Competition:

The best way to find out what could be successful for you is finding out what has been successful for others with products similar to yours. But always think out of the box, because you may have a better way to do it, one that will give you great results.

Learn what your competition is doing, what media they are using, and what results they are having. I always track between one month and three months, and I keep a record of everything that I see from my competition. At the end of the three months I can see how consistent they are, how their message may change to make it more successful, and I may also see changes in their strategy. Then if I look for the average I know if this particular media could work or not.

In the market that I have worked in Latin America lots of my competition used mass media advertising. However, it did not work for me very well. Even though I had sales from customers that I got from mass advertising, it was not the best media for me. I got better results doing events. Just know that you need to use whatever you're most comfortable working with and, most important, what gives you the greatest return on your investment of time and money.

Create a Plan to Succeed:

If you have seen me speak, you know that the most important thing I encourage people to have is a Plan, for whatever you want to do in life. If you want to be successful you need to have a plan that will give you the direction to get where you want to go. That will make a huge difference in the results you have in your professional life.

Finding the Motive (the reason Why)

Meaning of "motive":

If you look up the word "motive" in the dictionary you will find that it says "which moves," Motive is that which moves people to action. Finding Why you want to do Real Estate is critical in this process because if the Why is not strong enough, your success will be more a matter of luck. For a long time I have been amazed that when I ask *Why are you doing Real Estate or think you want to do it?*, most people don't even known a reason. With time, they quit because they find this business more difficult than what they thought. Without a reason Why that is strong enough, there is no reason to stay in the business and do what it takes to make it happen.

Why You Want to Do This:

You need to find your compelling reasons for doing this business. If you are thinking right now, "Yes, I have a compelling reason to do this: To make money," then you need to go deeper. What will the money give you that makes it so important to make money? In other words, you are doing this not to make money; you are doing this for what money will give you when you have it. The money is just the vehicle to get what you want (vacations, quality of life, financial freedom, etc.). Find the real reasons Why and write them down so you can see them every day or at least every time that you need to go back and focus. Your compelling reasons are the ones that move you to action, and action creates results.

List of Goals:

The first thing is to create a list of goals that you want to achieve. You will have short-term goals (6 months - 1 year), mid-term goals (1-3 years), and long-term goals (3 years and more). When you do a goal-setting exercise write goals that will be with you professionally and personally. Remember, your professional goals will be tied to your personal life, and if you found your Why I am sure that one of the main Whys has to do with achievement at the personal level. Do not make the mistake I did when I was 20 years old: All my professional goals were around my professional achievement until I got to the point that I did not have much of a personal life. I was leaving to the side my family and personal dreams until I was around 24 years old and realized that my life was a huge success at the professional level and a mess on the personal side. At that point I decided to start working on getting balance in my life, and that's when I understood that both the professional me and the personal me are parts of a whole. I started achieving more and have more sense of what being successful is. And even more important, I started to enjoy my life.

So put on some music that inspires you and start dreaming. Write all the goals that you have, no matter how small or big they are or how impossible they look now; just write them down. Remember to list the goals in all the roles in your life: physical, mental, spiritual, personal, professional.

Next, classify them as short-, mid- or long-term. Now you have your list of goals. Put them where you can review the list consistently. You can add more if you want to, and it always feels really good to cross one out when you've achieved it.

If you want to play more with this, create a "Dream Board" with pictures of your goals. Place it where you can see it every day. This will keep you motivated and help you move into action, as well as get back in focus when you need to. If you want to go deeper on "Goal-setting," read or listen to Stephen Covey's or Anthony Robbins' programs. I use them myself to keep focused, and I recommend them highly.

Taking Action

In all my years of working with sales agents, I have found that when the agent is an employee they comply to the action plans and achieve more easily the goals that the company sets for them. But, incredibly enough, when the same sales agent is an independent contractor it's harder for them to stick to an action plan, to reach their goals and to achieve success. After talking with several sales agents I found three main reasons why it is harder to succeed as an independent contractor: fear, procrastination and accountability.

Even though this is a book about strategies, you need to be aware that techniques are only a part of the equation. Your state of mind is the biggest part. If you read the stories, for example, about Donald Trump, Tiger Woods, or Robert Kiyosaki, you will see that the main component of their success is their ability of keep their state of mind in a place where they can create success. If you are one of those readers looking for tools, they are coming, but I would ask you to read this first and take it seriously.

Fear:

The saying "Knowledge is power" has been around for a long time, but now I hear more often "Action is power," and I agreed 100% with that statement. You can read thousands of books and go to one hundred seminars, but if you do not put into action what you learn and start making mistakes along the way, you won't reach your goals. What will make you successful is trial and error! I could tell you several classic examples, but I prefer to talk about my own experience with something that has nothing to do with business, but is real life and a simple reflection on how things work.

When I came to the US, the Food Network was my preferred television channel. I did not know how to cook more than the basics at that point. I watched for several months, and at one point I remember giving recipes and cooking tips to my friends, yet I was still not cooking for myself. I realized that I was so afraid of burning my food or that the taste would not be as good as it "should" be that I did not try. It was not until I started cooking, made mistakes, then began again and adjusted in light of what I learned the last time, that I finally learned how to cook.

Bottom line: You need to go out into the market and start by trial and error if you want to become successful in this business. I know that will cost you time and money, but I can tell you that becoming an expert and experienced in the field is what will make you successful. I like to say that *Failing is not an option for me, but making mistakes is part of the deal*, so be OK with that and start taking action now.

Procrastination:

Procrastination is a big one, and usually has to do with the fear of failing and fear of rejection. I have to tell you this now before you continue reading this book: Rejection is a huge part of the selling process. You need to get used to it and play with it, because if you want to be in the business of sales for the rest of your life you will have lots of NOs and you need to be strong enough to say *NEXT!*

People usually procrastinate because they do not want to deal with trial and error. Most of the time we are procrastinating because we are dealing with our own objections and excuses for why we did not do what we were supposed to.

Some of the most common objections and excuses that I hear in this market are:

– "I don't have the time." If this is your business, you have eight hours per day to work on this.

– "I don't have money to invest to get customers." Several marketing and sales activities do not require investment of big amounts of money and they also provide a high rate of return. Once you start selling, you need to save a percentage of the gains to re-invest into your business.

– "I have the money but I do not want to invest in my business." If that is the case, this may not be the career for you. You may be more comfortable having a job where you work for somebody else for a salary.

– "I don't know anyone in that market." There are several ways to start contacting people. Most of my customers didn't know me before I started working in this business. I found great ways to meet new people and reach potential customers that turned into sales. More about this in upcoming chapters.

– "I don't know how to start." First, know Why you want to do this and where you want to go, then make a plan and take action.

I remember the first Mike Ferry seminar that I went to. He said something like, "What do you want to make: money or excuses?" I thought that was brilliant because, in fact, we have the choice to hide behind the excuses and stay where we are, or take action, move forward and start making money.

Accountability:

As I shared before, when I talk with sales agents who are employees, they usually are successful at achieving their goals. So I was curious to find out how some sales agents can be more successful working for others than as independent contractors, especially if they have the same amount of hours. By the way, sales employees usually need to spend hours reporting what they did on their sales visits and calls, so the independent contractor actually has more time to invest on developing business.

The main difference I found is accountability. A Sales Agent who works for a salary is required to maintain a minimum sales quota and has to stick to a plan. If they do not achieve their goals, they are fired. On the contrary, independent sales agents do not have to be accountable to anyone. They usually have not set up a quota; or, if they have and they don't meet it, no one is fired.

This is where the Why plays an important role, because the Why is what is going to make you accountable to yourself. Some Real Estate Agents hire a coach so they can be accountable. Think about working in teams where you can have to be accountable, or hire a coach who can help you follow your plan and support you to do what you committed to.

Marketing

Marketing is important in any type of business, especially one like International Real Estate where there is so much competition.

Local Tools:

As I mentioned before, you need to decide which tools are available for your marketing, which ones have made other Real Estate Agents successful, and which ones you are comfortable using. Once you decide what tool(s) you are going to use, make sure that they align with your specialty. Sometimes using the wrong media can hurt your image, so be sure to choose what makes you be seen as a professional.

How to Get to Your Market Segment:

There are different ways to get to your target market. I have found that when I do direct selling I have more success than when I use mass media. Always evaluate the cost vs. results to find the percentage of effectiveness that a medium or activity has for you.

Let's say that you spend $10,000 on an advertising campaign that reaches 100,000 people. About ten people call you and you close one deal. On the other hand, you spend the same $10,000 to create an event where only fifty people show up and one person buys. Which medium is more effective?

In my point of view, the event was, because you got to be directly exposed to fifty potential customers, while with the advertising you got the attention of only ten. Also, with the advertising you had to end up in 100,000 hands to get one sale, and with the event you had to connect with only fifty people to get one sale. And with the event you have forty-nine potential customers you can work with in the future.

Always be looking for short-term and long-term results. I still have customers saying that they called me because they listened to one of my seminars X years ago. I get to close the sale of a marketing investment that I made a long time ago.

What Has Been Successful for Others

As you have read in this book, I like to research the competition because I believe that you don't need to make their mistakes. It also helps you create new things or do what they do better. I like the fast track to success, which means learning from the best, learning from their mistakes, getting the best from their experiences and becoming the best in what you do. You can check out other products that target the same segment of the market. Watch the best ones to understand what they are doing and why, and use what you learn to create a plan that aligns with your product.

Working with a Budget:

You need to know how much money you have to develop your plan. On the basis of that you can create something that will make sense for you. I know people who invest $4,000 on a monthly basis to promote their website on the Internet and they are successful in what they do, but what you need to look for is the return on investment. It is not how much you invest; it is how much money you get in return. I personally prefer to look at low-cost activities that produce the greatest results, and I focus on that consistently. Set up your budget before you start doing your marketing plan because you will need to work around your numbers.

Make a list of all the tools you are considering. Write the prices beside each. List the frequency and type of commitments; for example, some magazines ask you to sign a contract for several months. You need to brainstorm a list of everything you may want to use, then rank each one in order of importance, with #1s the most important; #2s are the ones you would like to do but maybe not now; #3s are the ones that you are not sure about. This list will give you an idea of how much money you need if you decide to do it all. Most likely you will take some things out that you do not need or don't plan for immediate action. Some numbers may look large for your budget, and that is fine; nobody is going to charge you for putting that on the brainstorming list. Just do it and later in your action plan you will decide what you are going to do and use.

Growing Strategy

One of the critical points when you start growing your business is having a strategy that supports the increased demand on you and your time.

Customer Service:

The key here is to be sure to deliver what you promise. A huge mistake that some companies make is that they get the marketing campaign out, but they are not prepared to support the demand. They get overwhelmed to the point that they fail on delivering the service they promised to their customers and potential customers. This is a great problem to have and very easy to solve, but you need to be prepared for this because if you are doing things right you will get to this point. I recommend creating a system to follow up each part of the process. Several software/ contact manager programs that will help you track your follow-ups are already on the market. One that I like a lot is "Top Producer" because it is specialized for Realtors®. You can edit it or customize it to suit your needs for your international customers.

Products:

What happened to me was that my customers got used to working with me, and when they start thinking about doing another type of Real Estate business they did not want to go with somebody else. So I created a team of professionals who work with me to get the customer what the customer needs. Remember at the beginning of the book when I said that I always say YES? Well, if your customer is asking you for something that is not your expertise, just find the right Real Estate Agent to join your team and do it. Real Estate Agents who are experts in other areas, markets or types of properties (products) can work with you whether they are in the same company or not. You can always work with referrals fees, and you are free to work with whomever you want as long as they have an active Real Estate License. Having a variety of products to offer is necessary to serve your international customers.

Markets:

My first business plan was to get into a new country every three months, and I have to confess that I was totally out of my mind when I thought that. Again it is trial and error, and I hope you learn from my mistakes. For a year I spent so much time and money "trying" to get into new markets that I started to ignore the market that I was getting strong in. That was a mistake, but when I realized what was going on I was able to make changes in my plan and make the plan work for me. What I do recommend is to create a strategy where you grow stronger in each market that you decide to get into. Some Agents have been successful getting into different markets at the same time, and if you choose to do that you need a team of people to support you. In a later chapter I will give you an overview of what to expect from a sales cycle.

If you are planning to expand your market, one way is to expand inside the country you're already in. For example, if you are working with Colombia you can create a growing strategy to get to a new city every X amount of time.

Support Team:

You need to build a team to deliver. Start considering this once you get at least four working customers per month, maybe sooner, depending on how much research work and in-house marketing you need. Sometimes outsourcing is cheaper, sometimes not, so analyze what works best for you.

A support team could consist of an assistant, closing coordinator, and other Real Estate Agents who work with your leads, showings, and other Real Estate activities. If you are considering working with different countries, the best way is with a team of Real Estate Agents, each specialized in a country, so each market gets the attention it needs to become strong.

Investment vs. Income:

Keep control of what you are investing and how much money you are making so you can evaluate the return on your investments. I have stopped marketing to one particular country because the results did not justify continuing. I reallocated the budget assigned to that market to another country that, with a lot less investment, was giving me huge results. Remember, it is not how much you make, it is how much you get in return for what you invest.

Find Customers

How do I find customers? This is the No. 1 question that I get every time I coach Real Estate Agents. I will be talking about some common methods but there are still more, and if you are successful already doing something, do not stop doing it! This book is to teach you new things but also to help you get better in what is giving you good results. You may want to take one or a few things from here to get even better. You do not need to do ALL at one time. I encourage you to choose two or three activities, see what happens, then become an expert on the ones that give you the best results.

Networking:

Every tip I have leads to one main tip: <u>TALK to people!</u>

Notice what just happened with you when you read that line. Did you have butterflies in your belly? Did you think, "OMG, I don't like this anymore!"? Or are you feeling excited about how easy this can be? If you have the butterflies, that's OK; it's part of the deal. All of us have a fear of rejection and as I mentioned before you are going to have lots of NOs until you get a YES. So if you want to get into sales, or you are already in sales, you have to deal with it. It is part of our profession.

If you thought, "OMG, I don't like this anymore!" and maybe you felt like running to the bathroom, I recommend that you think about how important international Real Estate sales are for you. And if you still do not feel like doing it, you may want to go for another career because there is no way you can sell if you do not talk to people.

If you are totally excited about talking to people, just hold onto your horses and create a strategy before you do so. Some people get so excited that they start talking like crazy with potential customers and scare them away instead of attracting them. These agents don't have a system so they talk, talk, talk but don't do anything else because they don't have a plan for what to do next.

If you look at the basics of networking, you'll realize that you network every day. Think right now about how many people you talked with yesterday. Or maybe today, if you are reading this book at the end of the day, I bet that you talked to a minimum of three to five people: The guy from the coffee shop; the waitress at the restaurant where you got lunch; your co-worker in the office right next to you; the security guy at the office building or where you live; maybe you talked to a friend or two over the phone. You are already talking with people every day; now how can you take advantage of this for going international? What I do every time I am planning to travel is I speak with everyone – YES, everyone – who crosses my path. I tell them that I am excited that I am traveling to whatever country it is to sell Real Estate, and I ask if they know someone who lives there or someone in the US who may have family or people that they know in that country. I do the same thing with the people at work, other colleagues that may not work internationally, or maybe they do but they are not traveling right now and may want me to contact their customers. I also contact other professionals, like lawyers, accountants, mortgage brokers, and I always end up with a few appointments from the referrals that all these people give me.

The best advice I can give you here is to not leave anyone out because you think they cannot afford to buy what you are offering. A few years ago I was referred to a woman who was a secretary in Venezuela, and I presumed that she could not afford to buy property in Miami because it was totally out of her income range. But she put me in contact with her boss, and her boss got one property from me. And few years later she called to let me know that she and her husband were coming to Miami and were interested in buying property here. You never know who could be your next customer, so do not presume anything. Treat everyone like a potential customer.

The best way to start using your network of people you already know is to create a list of at least 100 people. And if you are thinking, "I don't know that many people in the whole world," I am sure that is not true. Come on, you know more people than you think! Put on that list __ALL__ the people that you have had contact with in the last two years, and then start calling them and telling them what you are doing and ask for referrals. If you do this every day for at least one hour per day or a minimum of 10 contacts per day, you will have your business up and running very soon. Actually, sooner than you think.

Referrals from Professionals:

Another way that works really well is going to other Real Estate Agents in the US who can refer you to their potential customers in the country you're going to. You may be asking, "Why would they refer those customers to me?" The truth is that a lot of customers like one-on-one presentations, meeting the person at the other end of the phone, and many local Real Estate Agents lose business because they do not travel and do not take the time to show their faces and connect personally with their customers. Also, you have to network with local Real Estate Agents they can set up appointments for you with their customers. More about this in a later chapter.

Referrals from Customers:

The best referrals are your past customers. Even though they are local customers they may know people all over the world, and if they are happy with your work they will be more than happy to refer you to their friends and potential customers.

Walk Your Dog:

I have to mention this here because you need to think out of the box! There are activities that you are already doing which will give you business if you have a strategy, and something simple like walking your dog is one way to do it. About four years ago I met a Realtor® I thought was really good at what he was doing, and when I asked him what his marketing activities were, he said that he walks his dog for about two hours per day. Everybody in his community knew about him, he stopped and talked to everyone, and 100% of his customers come from them. So think about what you already are doing—sports, entertainment, church—and use your contacts to develop your international business.

Using the Internet to Reach Customers

A great way to get in contact with international customers is using the tools that the Internet provides. Just remember, this is a numbers game, and you will have to reach lots of people before you can get to close a sale, and in some cases you will work with customers that end up buying with another Real Estate Agent.

Website:

If you are going to be or already are working with international customers, having a website is a must. You need a place where people can go and have service from you 24/7. There are many ways that you can use your website to capture potential customers, but first make sure that your website name is everywhere: on your business cards, emails, everything that you give or send to the people that you connect with. It is also key to drive people to your website so you can create a database that you will use consistently to promote your services.

One of the most important things is to keep your website up to date, adding new stuff and new information so people will be interested in going back to see what's new. Your website needs to be active if you want people to come back, and if you want it to rise in the rankings assigned by the search engines.

Blogging:

Creating a blog is a great way to put your name out there as an expert in the field. Just make sure you are prepared to deal with any type of people getting into your discussions. You will have people who believe this is the business to be in, and some will just give you all the reasons why people should not buy Real Estate. You have to be prepared to respond to any of that.

Newsletter:

The key thing with newsletters is consistency. Some people send a newsletter every two weeks, some once per month, some once every two months. Be respectful of people, so do not spam. Make short articles and be accurate in the information that you send. You are in the public eye now and you want to make sure that your message is worth reading and keeps you out of their spam folder.

Email Marketing:

Email is great to promote special events, new products on the market, hot deals, etc., and the response is almost immediate. Usually people read emails and respond or erase them, and a few save them to take a look later or forward to someone else.

With email marketing just make sure that your recipients subscribe to your website or are people you met. Ask permission to add them to your mailing list. If you spam, it will only be a matter of time before you get complaints, or your email address will be reported, and your mailings will go directly to the spam folder in some of the emails servers. Email is a powerful tool, so please use it wisely.

Advertising

Measuring Your Results:

When you do advertising, make sure that you have a way to register the results so you can evaluate what is giving you the best outcome. When you go to mass media, you are hitting the cold market and the response there will be lower in percentage than what you get when you work in direct advertising, like sending a letter to a target who is more likely to buy internationally.

Advertising is just one component of the marketing process. I have seen companies that have a great response from an advertising effort, but they do not answer calls or emails on time, or they do not deliver what they promise or they do not close the deal. Advertising gets the potential customer interested, and it is your job to take him by the hand and guide him.

Cost vs. Benefits:

The advertising effort is measured by the immediate response that the ad, or piece, generates. Always have a phone number or an email address where people can respond, or direct them to your website. If you have several activities going on, I recommend that you create special email addresses where people can respond. If the customer contacts you by phone, you can always ask, "How did you find out about us?"

When you measure results you also want to measure the quality of the results. To give you an example, if you place an ad in a local newspaper and twenty people contact you but none are qualified to buy, then something is wrong with the message in the ad. You need to pre-qualify your potential customers to see how successful the message is in getting to the right target.

Knowing the results that each activity generates will give you an idea of cost vs. benefits and then you can decide what are the most profitable media to use. Also register the amount of time it takes to get a response from each medium, so you have an idea of what to expect the next time you design an action plan.

Sales is a numbers game, and advertising and marketing have to be with the first part of the cycle of sales. Play with the numbers and create a strategy that allows you to be more assertive and have a better return on your investment.

Events

This is what I like the most, because I get to talk with people and they get to know my face. Besides, you become more successful when people know you and like you.

How to Get the Most:

When I started working for the major hotel chain, I asked one of the Regional Managers what was the best advice he could give me to be great in sales. He said, "Become the fastest business card-giver on the earth," and he was right. I gave away about 250-500 cards per month. I was giving cards to everyone, and at the end of the year everyone knew who I was. That gave me credibility and sales, and soon promotions to higher positions. You have to become a business card-giver and make sure that you always have enough cards with you. It is horrible when someone asks for your business card and you have to say that you don't have any more.

Also ask for others' business cards. Some people will tell you that they do not have any more, so be prepared – bring a little notepad so they can give you their information. The most important thing you want from them is an email address, because that's the easiest way to be connected. The next day, send them a short email with your contact info, as a reminder and just in case your business card ended up in the trash before they got to their PDA or computer.

You can make this activity fun. I go with one or two colleagues, and we compare at the end of the night how many business cards we got, or we set up a minimum goal and whoever loses buys dinner. Setting up a minimum goal gives you a clear strategy so you will start taking the time to build a relationship with someone you just met. Please don't become that Real Estate Agent who stays with the same two people the whole night. That is NOT networking!

If you go with more people from your team, a great thing to do is to introduce your colleague to someone new, then you go meet someone else while your colleague stays with the person they just met. Then your colleague will do the same for you, so someone is always talking with someone new and people get to meet more people from your team.

If you go to an event with someone who knows everyone, ask that person to take the first 30 minutes to introduce you to the most people he can, then you go around connecting with those people.

Networking Events:

There are different types of networking events, and the dynamics change a little bit. The key to networking events is that everyone goes with the same mission, which is to meet people, so you will see that people are walking around introducing themselves and giving and taking business cards like crazy. This is a great opportunity to meet people, so make sure that you bring tons of business cards, and even have extras in your car. Some networking events offer the possibility to rent a space to promote your product. Don't waste your money renting a space unless you have a specific product such as a pre-construction project or land.

If you are traveling to a country to develop your international business, find out if there is any networking event happening during your visit. Also find out in your hometown if the community that represents the country you are targeting has a Chamber of Commerce or other institutions in charge of developing commercial opportunities between the two countries. They will be more than glad to invite you to their events so you can start connecting with potential customers, or people who can refer business to you, or potential liaisons.

Seminars:

It is a great idea if you feel comfortable to give seminars to your potential customers. Just make sure that you have a wide knowledge of how Real Estate works in their country, because the audience will tend to compare the US system with theirs. You want to know what they are talking about when they ask questions. Also make sure to not use slang if you are not 100% sure what it means. Some things may have different meanings in different countries, or different meanings depending on the context.

Another option is to be invited as a guest speaker in a seminar that others organize. Again, stepping in front of an audience requires a lot of responsibility so make sure that you are knowledgeable about your topic because you always will get questions.

Cocktail Events:

I love the concept of the napkin presentation. Learn how to make a napkin presentation in less than ten minutes, so you can get the attention of potential customers with a short speech then follow up after the event with a more formal meeting. Most people at cocktail parties talk about business, so it is a safe environment to prospect. Just be smart in the way that you do it. Do not use the "me, me, me" technique because your listener will run away. Ask questions first, be interested in the person you are meeting, create rapport and then talk a little bit about how you help people by doing what you do. Most people do not like to be sold, so if you have a sales pitch this is not the moment to use it. You will have better results when you talk about what you are doing for others.

Social Events:

Going to parties and meeting people can have a new whole meaning if you take this opportunity to make contacts and develop relationships that could transform into business later. Once I heard in a sales seminar that "People do business with people they know, like and trust." In social events you will find that some people don't talk much about business. My recommendation in this case is get to know the person and then call them after the event and make a business call or set up an appointment.

Do's and Don'ts

OK, here is where I am going to be a little bit annoying, but I have seen lots of things, and everything I am saying here is based on my experience, so take it or leave it!

Personal Touch:

This might be inappropriate in some countries, like Japan, but in others it is the way people connect. For example, in Argentina when people meet they kiss on the cheek as part of the introduction. In Spain they give two kisses, one on each cheek. Learning the customs will help you align better with your customer. Find out about the business etiquette in the country you are targeting. There are tons of websites that talk about this, so google "international etiquette," or even look for the country. A website I go to often for tips about international etiquette is http://www.executiveplanet.com.

Politics and Religion:

If you don't know the customer well, I strongly suggest avoiding those topics. Some countries are going through complicated political situations so you don't want to talk about subjects that might make your customer feel uncomfortable.

Drinking:

If you choose to drink alcohol, limit yourself to what you know will keep your professional image. Don't get into a state where you become the joke of the night, or at least become so annoying that the next day people won't answer your calls. I have been asked by some of my students what to do when they feel the pressure of drinking because the organizer is giving them drinks, or they are in those situations where they cannot say No. Well, just take the glass, take a sip and then walk around. If you get tired of that glass, put it away and later take another one and do the same. If you need to have a glass in your hand, you can do it without drinking so much that it gets you in trouble. During business cocktails some people get so drunk that they talk without stopping, they become disrespectful, and I even have seen at an exclusive event a woman peeing herself in the middle of the room in front of the top executives in the city. Even though that happened more than thirteen years ago, my colleagues and I remember. If you choose to drink, do it knowing your limitations, because you want to look professional all the time.

Smoking:

Some countries have rules about not smoking in some places, but I have found that most of the countries outside the US do not have strict rules about this. If you smoke just make sure to ask before you light a cigarette, as a show of respect.

Jokes:

Be careful with this one. Some words have different meanings in different countries even though they share the same language. And some cultures are not very open to your being playful with someone in a business environment, so instead of helping you, joking could harm your image. In my experience, when an Agent uses a joke to lower tension or break the ice with international customers, it's usually not understood or well received. You can create rapport with a light conversation, so don't take the risk of offending the other party by the wrong use of a word.

Dress:

Some countries are more formal, some more casual. Make sure before you start your trip to find out what the business dress etiquette is in that country. You want to be in tune with their culture and not be overdressed or too casual. I remember walking the streets of Curaçao in a sales blitz, wearing high heels, a skirt and a business jacket in 80-degree weather, and most of my customers were in shorts and sandals. I was totally overdressed for the occasion. And yes, I learned that researching how people dress for business is important before I travel.

Confidentiality:

A lot of international customers are investing in the US because they feel safer here than in their own country. I have worked with people from Colombia, Venezuela and Argentina that are afraid of others' knowing that they have money because they are afraid of kidnapping. People want to invest for different reasons. It is a must that you keep private any personal information they share with you. Do not share that information with other customers. About four years ago I met a mortgage broker specializing in international customers who offered his services to me so I could refer him to my customers who were looking for a loan. The interview I had with him was great, until in the middle of it he started talking about his customers, giving names and saying things about them that I am sure they did not want discussed in a meeting with anyone else. One of the names he mentioned was a person I knew well from Venezuela. When he finished talking I said that I could not work with him because I lost my trust in him.

CHAPTER 3
WHO ARE YOUR POTENTIAL CUSTOMERS?

Defining Your Target Market

Understanding the Potential Customer:

Each customer you work with is going to be different. If you want to become a successful International Real Estate Agent, one of the most important things is to have repeat business. To get that, develop rapport with your customer and the customer is happy. Everything starts with understanding the customer's needs, and for that you need to become a master at asking questions.

Find out why they want to invest. That will give you a sense of how important this is for them and whether they are serious or not about buying property in the US. Ask for their goals. You may find that what they want may not be achievable, and no matter how well you do your job the customer won't be happy. If their goals are not realistic, it is your job to explain the reality of the market. I met a customer in 2005 who told me that his goal was buy a property then immediately put it back on the market and resell it for double the price. If you were in Real Estate in 2005, you know that flipping property immediately for double the price was almost impossible, even though the Real Estate market was going up fast due the high demand of buyers seeking properties. When I told him that his plan was not realistic in the current market, he mentioned that he had a friend who did it all the time, so he ended up partnering with his friend to buy and re-sell. A year later he said that he could not make any money in the houses that he got with his friend. Even though they resold them at a higher price, he had to pay for repairs, commissions, lawyers, taxes, etc. In the end, the real profit for him was less than 10%. He was so upset that he told me he would never buy in the US again. In other words, a customer who has false expectations won't get his needs satisfied and will go back to his country and tell others that it is not good to do business in the US.

When you talk the first time also get clear about what the customer wants short-term and long-term, and help them develop a plan that is aligned with those realities, as best you can predict them. Always be conservative. Giving high expectations is not a good idea.

Ask them about their past experience buying property in the US. If they do not have any, ask if they have bought property anywhere in the world. See what their experience has been, the good ones and the bad ones, because the experiences that happened in the past are coming with them. After they share with you, I recommend that you tell them what you have experienced in similar cases here in the US where the outcomes were different, so they are prepared to see a different approach or even a different result.

Listening Is Key:

The most successful sales agents in today's market are those who listen to what the customer has to say, instead of talk, talk, talk. The potential customer will become your customer because they find value working with you, not because of who you are. Customers will work with you because of what you can do for them.

In this era, business is about the customer, and we as professionals have to find the way to deliver what the customers are looking for. If that is something we cannot deliver, it is better to refer them to someone who has the tools or knowledge so you don't lose the customer. Maybe you are thinking right now that referring the customer is losing the customer. Well, not in my point of view. When you refer the customer you are still in contact with them, and believe me, the customer will be very happy if you refer them to someone who does a great job. You will lose the customer if you don't deliver. The customer will get upset and walk away from you to work with someone else who is not in partnership with you, and you lose your share of the commission. That is losing the customer.

Reading Body Language:

When you listen to your customer make sure that you are listening with your ears and eyes, because body language says much more than words. You may see things that will help you understand how the customer feels or reacts to the different properties that you are presenting. If you get good at reading people, you will be successful in this business.

Asking Powerful Questions:

As you have read, I believe in asking questions. That's because each of us has different realties and the only way to know what a customer thinks about something is to ask questions and listen to what they have to say. Here's the deal: If you ask questions, it will be easier to do business because the customer has all the answers for you to close the deal. They will tell you everything. Use the following questions in meeting with your customers, and remember that questions may change based on what the customer is interested in, or on the information they have given you already.

Some of the powerful questions I ask are:

➢ What do you plan to do with the property?

➢ For how long are you planning to keep the property?

➢ What percentage or return on investment is your goal? What is the minimum you would be happy with? (Even though you predict a percentage, knowing what the customer is looking for helps you determine if it's achievable or not.)

➢ Are other persons involved in the decision?

➢ When are you going to make the decision?

➢ What is a must-have in the property?

➢ How much money do you have available to invest in the property?

➢ What is your main goal for having this property? (If they are looking for a vacation property the decision-making process will be different than if they are looking for an income property, or if they are looking for a primary residence.)

➢ If we find the right property for you in the next few days, how much time do you need to be able to close? (If the customer won't be ready to close for another three months, the negotiations with the seller will be different than if the buyer is ready to close in the next ten days.)

➢ Is this your first time buying in the US? If not, what was your experience in the past?

Those are some of the questions I like to ask. You want to ask open-ended questions so you can understand what the customer is looking for. Sometimes even they are not clear on what they want.

Potential Real Estate Liaisons

What They Expect:

Your liaisons are your business partners, people who refer clients to you. As stakeholders they need to know what you expect, but at the same time you need to know what they expect.

Usually they are looking for service, fast response, and that the customer they refer to you is being taken care of during the entire selling process.

Also they expect that the Real Estate Agent in the US will stick to the agreement so they get paid and on time. One of the main complaints I hear from international liaisons is that they send referrals to Real Estate Agents in the US who then close the sale, but they never get paid, or they do not get paid the figure that was agreed upon. Be careful with this one; you can get a bad reputation. Usually the Real Estate communities in other countries are smaller than here and they spread the word very easily. To give you an example, in each seminar I have given where someone shares about something that happened, they also share the name of the person and the company involved, and I see that the rest of the participants write that down.

I like to have written agreements so everyone is on the same page and knows what to expect. I strongly recommend the TRC (Transnational Referral Certified) certification from the International Consortium of Real Estate Associations (ICREA) http://www.worldproperties.com. Use the tools they offer their members because they go over these agreements, they provide you with documents, and they promote agreement between Real Estate Boards in different countries. Therefore, if you are doing business with a country that is on their list and a dispute happens, you can go to mediation with ICREA support. That helps resolve any dispute on the best terms. At the same time, being a member of this organization will give you recognition and credibility on the international market.

Keep your international liaison informed while you are working with their customer. They want to know what's going on, which step you are on, and sometimes they may be a great help if the customer is making the decision in their country. Also make sure that if the customer calls you in the future asking for your service again, you let your liaison know and recognize the agreement. Some Brokers or Real Estate Agents won't agree with me on this one, but I can tell you that in my experience if you do not recognize them they will never send you a customer again and, what is worse, will give you a bad reputation. If the policy in your company is different, make sure that you make that clear to your liaison from the beginning, and that it is in writing, to prevent any misunderstanding.

The International Real Estate Professional

Referral Agreements:

When you make an agreement with an International Real Estate Professional, define how much referral commission you are going to pay. Some companies have a policy already in place; others have not worked with international referrals before. If that is the case, ask your Broker to give you permission to deal with that and to give you parameters. Each country is different, so do your research. The best way to know how much to pay is to ask the International Real Estate Agent, "How much do you pay as a referral if I send you a customer?" That will tell you what he would be willing to give, which may also be what he would expect to receive. I say "willing" because I have been in different situations, one so ridiculous that I could not work with the person. I asked him how much he would pay me as a referral if I sent him a customer, and he responded, "Twenty-five percent." When I sent him the written agreement I put in that he would receive a 25% referral fee for the customers he sent to the US. He called me back and said that he wouldn't refer for less than 40%. In that case I decided to say Bye-bye! When you choose with whom you want to work, be sure it's a win-win situation.

I am very clear on the agreement about when we get paid. Sometimes the customer buys a preconstruction project and the project pre-pays part of the commission, and sometimes they pay the whole amount at closing. I recommend that you explain how the payment process works so they know what you expect.

I have a payment structure depending on the type of referral. Sometimes the Real Estate Agent in another country refers customers who are pretty much ready to buy and may even buy over the phone and by mail. But most of the time the customer comes to the US and needs to be taken care of—pick them up at the airport, drive them around to show the properties. Also, I have a different structure of commissions depending on whether the customer buys pre-construction, a re-sale or commercial. Each type of business is different and requires different investments of time.

I want to make clear to the agent referring the customer to me that I have a confidentiality agreement with the customer and I won't share their information with them. I explain how this works and why confidentiality is important with International customers. I ask the same from them. If the customer chooses to share any information with them I ask the agent to keep it confidential as part of our responsibility to the customers.

I like to make agreements that are bilateral so if I have a customer interested in buying in that country I will be able to refer the customer to the agent and receive the same treatment that their referral is getting from me.

One of the things that I ask of my international business partners is that they respect the process we must follow in the US, and I ask them to not interfere. I am very strict about this because we have a Real Estate License in the US which is totally different than in other countries. Most other countries do not have rules, laws or a code of ethics to follow like we have here. I have had many cases where I am working with a customer and the International Real Estate Agent talks to him and says things that he heard from another person or that he believes for some reason, and the agent creates a misunderstanding with the customer that can cost the sale. Even worse, we may close the sale but then the customer has future problems because of that misunderstanding.

Choosing the Right Professional:

To avoid problems, choose to work with professionals. The best way is to interview them and decide which one is more aligned with what you are looking for in their style of doing business, experience, ethics, contacts, etc.

Make a list of the characteristics that an International Real Estate Agent must have in order to work with you. When you interview them, make sure to stick to the list. Mark each item in your list as either "must have" or "great if they have it," so you are clear what is negotiable and what is not. If they don't have what is negotiable, that's fine; you may still work with them. But if they don't have what is a must-have, you know from the beginning that this is not someone you can work with. The best example I can give you is this: I met with the manager of a real estate group in Venezuela who wanted to send me customers. We talked about a month and got to the point that we were ready to sign the agreement. Then the people who organize my seminars invited him to attend one of them. When he called me a couple of days after the seminar, letting me know that he had his first customer to refer to me, I realized that this man had been prospecting my customers at my seminar! I choose to cancel the agreement and stop working with that real estate group.

Having rapport with your liaisons is important, but also notice the rapport they have with their customers. It will show you how they will treat potential customers that you may send to buy in their market.

Learning How to Work with International Real Estate Agents:

Take the time to learn from different sources how to work with international customers. One of the best sources are the seminars that the NAR® and the Boards of Realtors® offer. Visit www.Realtor.org to find more info about the CIPS (Certified International Property Specialist) and http://www.worldproperties.com for the TRC. Call your local association and ask about what they have available for International Realtors.®

International Real Estate Agents in the US with International Customers

A lot of business comes directly from other US Realtors® who don't work with international customers, or from International Real Estates Agents from other cities who want to refer their customers to Realtors® who know how to work with International Customers.

Go to International events, locally and internationally, and you will get to know lots of Real Estate Agents. Any one of them could be a great contact for referring customers to your area. At the same time you will meet lots of Real Estate Agents to whom you can refer your business.

Call your local Board of Realtors® and ask if they have an International council or committee, and ask them about the events that they may have or recommend. Some Boards organize or promote International missions to foreign countries. If they are going to the country that you want to work with, you may want to take that opportunity, especially if you don't know anyone in that country. Just know that if you go on a mission with twenty other Realtors®, everyone is going to be prospecting, so make sure you clearly understand the goal for the trip and run the numbers to see if the investment in time and effort will be worth it.

Go to www.Realtor.org and look for the International events that NAR® is promoting, and attend the ones that make sense to you. They have several events during the year and it could be worth it if you want to meet other Realtors® who work with International Real Estate customers. NAR® has different types of events, such as conventions, roundtables, seminars, international missions, etc. The best way to be involved is to get your CIPS.

Other Professional Liaisons

There are several professionals who could be great sources of referrals for you because they work with your potential customers already.

Who They Are:

Real Estate and immigration lawyers, accountants, financial advisors, mortgage brokers, travel agencies, the bank, the concierge or bell boy at the hotels, etc. Any type of business that specializes or has constant contact with the international customer could be sending you potential customers.

Where to Find Them:

You can meet them in networking events, Chambers of Commerce, Real Estate events, social events, or ask your broker for the professionals that the company works with, then contact them. When you talk to this professional about the possibility of referring you business, remember that they are looking for the same. Basically this profession is all about referrals.

What They Expect:

They are expecting you to refer customers to them also. They want to be recognized by the experts in the Real Estate field and have the opportunity to work with them. Just remember that we cannot compensate anyone who does not have a Real Estate license, so make that clear to avoid problems or misunderstandings.

You need to have a team of experts for your customers. You can invite lawyers, accountants, mortgage brokers, etc., to be part of that support team. Interview them the same way you interview a Real Estate Agent you want to partner with, so you are sure that you are referring your customers to the best people.

A great way to work together is to create events or seminars to educate the customers in every part of the Real Estate process.

CHAPTER 4
WHERE IS YOUR MARKET?

Defining Your Market

Focus on Your Target Market:

At the beginning of the book I talked about being a strong believer in diversification, which I am, but you need to do it with a strategy that allows you to help your business instead of jeopardize it.

I have found that when you focus on one market you get better results in the early stages because you concentrate your efforts, time and money on that market. As I shared before, I tried to "conquer" several markets in a short period of time and it did not work as I expected. I realized that if I spent enough time in the market that I chose I could create a base that would allow me to grow over time and also allow me to expand to new markets without the risk of losing what I already had.

How long you may want to work on one specific market before you go to a new one depends on the results you are having and how much effort you are putting there. I recommend no less than six months to a year of working in a market before you start on a new one. This is based on my own experiences and that of Realtors® I have worked with.

Some of the benefits of focusing on a specific market are that you get recognized as an expert there, and the recognition brings you more business. At the same time, all the experience that you gain while working with a market helps you be much smarter and more efficient when you open the next one.

If you choose to focus on multiple markets, you can lose consistency in all of them, and consistency is important for the customers and for your business partners. As a consequence you may lose business because opening a new market requires a lot of time, and if you don't invest the necessary time you could burn all your bridges.

It's a Numbers Game

Selling is a numbers game, and depending on how long you have being selling Real Estate you may already be getting results with your current business. International Real Estate is not very different than what you are doing now. When you start working with international customers, you will find out what your numbers are; in other words, how many customers you need to contact before you get to close a sale. That will give you an idea when you plan for prospecting. In my experience, if you specialize in International Real Estate you may have a higher closing rate than you have in your local market. I believe that's because there are not as many agents competing with you internationally.

Your Strengths:

You need to identify your strengths and how they are going to support you in developing a market. For example, if you were born in X country and you have contacts there who can help you start promoting your business, that is a strength. Make a list of at least ten things you consider strengths that will help you develop your target market.

Growing Strategy:

Establish a timeline and stick to it in the development of the business so you have a goal based on how much time you will invest before you see results. Also, you may want to establish a routine. Let's say you want to develop your business with customers from Ecuador. How many times per year you will need to go there, how much money will you need to invest, what types of activities will you need to do and what frequency? In order to have an efficient growing strategy you need to consider many factors, but the most important are that you know what you want, why and what actions will take you there. More about growing strategy in the following chapters.

Consistency Is the Key:

After all these years of working with sales and international markets in different companies, representing different types of products, I have to say that the most important thing I've discovered about myself and other top producers has been the value of consistency. I remember watching the Tour de France the last year that Armstrong raced. The difference between him and the rest of the cyclists was that he was consistent; he was not winning every day but he was, overall, the most consistent cyclist. Being consistent will bring you success in your international Real Estate business.

Basics for Choosing Your Market

Choosing the right market to work on could make the difference between your being successful or failing.

Facts:

Some of the things you need to take into consideration are the facts about your target market. You need to know what's going on there that is making people buy. If it is a seasonal happening, you really need to evaluate how much effort you want to put in there. Make sure it is worth investing time and money. You want to look for opportunities that will give you business for the long term.

Language:

Language can be a factor in deciding which market works for you. If you speak Spanish, you may want to target a Spanish-speaking country. However, I have seen great sales people who develop markets where they do not speak the language. They use translators and are very successful. But in my opinion, it is more convenient when you can control your business and you don't need to depend on a translator to communicate.

Potential Allies:

It is convenient to know people in other countries because they can open doors in a way that will make it easier to see results in a short period of time.

Travel Availability:

In my opinion travel this is a must if you want to develop a strong international business. People like to meet the person that they are dealing with, and if you want to be in this business for a long time, traveling is part of it. At the beginning, when you start developing one particular niche, you have to travel with more frequency than when you have spent time working there and people already know you.

Working Your Niche:

You need to develop your niche in light of your strengths. The more unique you are, the better, because that will set you apart from the competition. If you find a little town in a country that shows interest in what you have to offer, you may get into a gold mine. A colleague just went to a small town in a Latin American country and made a presentation to ten farmers. He closed nine of the ten, and the next month he is returning to meet with a new group that was referred by the first group.

Look for those key things that will make the difference. That will make you successful and encourage the customers to go with you instead of your competition.

Key Things about Your Market

Language:

Language is not simply the native language of the country. When I say *language* it is also about how they speak -- the idioms, the nuances, the words peculiar to your target country.

Culture:

Knowing the culture of your target country will make you more successful when you do presentations, business meetings, and closings. Each country does business differently. If you understand how, you will be able to adapt to their business culture, and that will give you even better results.

Income:

When you want to work in an international city, know what the median income is and what percentage of the population could afford to buy in your area. A few years ago I was researching the possibility of going to a country in Latin America to do events and take with me information about some preconstruction projects. When I did my research, though, I realized that the market which could afford what I offered was so small that it was not worth it to invest time and money promoting my business there. I decided to put the same effort in a market that had more potential customers.

Knowing the target market's income range, you can determine the potential range of investment. If they make enough money to invest, you have a wider range of opportunities. You will be able to offer a variety of products, and the selling process will be smoother. You may end up working with investors who buy and sell on a regular basis.

Trends:

The trends of a particular market offer a clue to what you can expect for the next two to five years. Even though we don't have crystal balls, we see our market growing or slowing down, depending on the reasons why people are buying, how they are buying, and what are they talking about. Being able to predict what could happen with your market in the next two to five years will give you the power to grow your business. The more stable your business is, the better, because you want to built a long-term relationship with your target market.

Why Choose a Specific Market:

There are so many reasons why a Real Estate Agent will choose to work with a specific market, and there is no right or wrong here. Make a list of why you should choose a particular market, and make sure you do it for reasons that make good business sense.

Some reasons are:

Proximity – Usually the countries closest to the US do business in the US. Proximity will also be more convenient in terms of travel expenses and time invested.

Relationship with that country – if you were born or raised outside the US, that country could be a great place to start doing business, especially if you already understand the culture and know the language. You will have even better results if you still have contacts there.

Knowledge – You may have worked with a country doing another type of business, or already have contacts there for some reason. If you know the country and the people, that is a great start.

Networking – Maybe you did business with people in that country in the past, or some local people you know are from that country and can refer you to others. Remember, this is a referral-based business, so the more people you know who can refer you business in that country, the better.

Past experience – If you have worked with someone from that country, it is OK to ask for referrals. Because they have already experienced your work habits and ethics, they'll be able to talk with their friends and families about you and be trusted.

Other people are doing it – This is not a strong reason for doing business internationally. I have seen lots of Real Estate Agents fail because they want to do business where they don't know anyone and don't know the country. They just wasted lots of money and time without any results.

There are lots of buyers buying in my area from that country – Again, maybe there are thousands of people from X country buying in your area, but what percentage you are going to get? And how much effort will you need to put into that market before you get a piece of it? My recommendation is to start where you have some type of connection that will lead you to potential customers.

CHAPTER 5
BUILDING A STRONG CASE

Getting Support From Your Broker

Most Brokers are open to develop international business if they think the time they invest to do that will be worth it. Some of them want to be involved; some will give you the green light and you take care of the rest with their full support.

Communicate:

Before you start developing your international business, talk to your broker and understand his/her thoughts in that regard. Tell your Broker what your goals are because those will affect the company. Your efforts will create more sales for them and expose the name of the company at the international level in the countries where you decide to work. Ask for support from your Broker. The type of support you are looking for could be access to their international referrals, developing a team with other potential international Realtors®, or even monetary support for events, international advertising and promotions. If your Broker sees you are serious about this business development, they are likely to give you support.

Share you plan with them and you might even ask them to participate in the planning process. And if your Broker does not have an International Division yet, this could be a great opportunity for you to create it.

Ask your Broker about experience in international markets they may have had in the past as a company or maybe as a sales agent. Learn from their good and bad experiences. You may discover that they had different results from what you can bring to the table with your experience and your contacts.

Agreements:

If the company you are working with already has experience with international markets, they may have agreements in place that you can use. If they do not have an agreement, or the one they have is not appropriate, you will have to create one.

When you sign an agreement with an International Broker, make sure that your Broker signs also, so they will be committed to it and everybody will be on the same page. Always keep a copy of the agreement and give your Broker a copy too. This way you make sure that if, for some reason, you leave that company before they get the commission, they will still honor the agreement to the International Broker. Therefore, your relationship with that International Broker won't be affected and you can go on to do more referral business with them.

Sponsorship:

There are many ways your Broker can serve as a sponsor when you do business internationally. You may want to ask for sponsorship to pay partial or total costs of the events you are going to develop in that country. Sometimes Brokers assign a budget to develop a market; sometimes they are willing to co-sponsor some of the events; or they may help you find a sponsor from their providers or developers who work with their company. Always ask for help. The worst thing that can happen is that they say no, but if they say yes that will give you resources to develop a market faster.

Policies and Procedures

My first experience when I started working internationally was a bit disappointing because when I told my Broker about the events I planned, he plugged another Realtor® into my marketing effort and made me split my efforts with this person. I was supposed to include this agent in every event I was doing. It was a small community where everybody knew each other. Some of my guests knew this person already. Instead of us working together, at one point we started competing against each other, which was not good for us, for our relationship with our potential customers, or for the company. So get clear before you make any agreement how things are going to work with your Broker. You don't want surprises after you do a lot of work.

It is important that you respect the policies and procedures of the company you work for. Because you are representing your company while in the relationship with your International Brokers, you want to make sure that the relationship follows the rules of your company. Let your team that is working with international customers knows about this. Include the policies and procedures of your company on the international agreement so everyone is informed. Be firm about following the rules.

Developing an International Division:

Ask your Broker if they have an International Division. If they do, make sure to become part of that team and align with them. They may have lots of experience already in what you want to do, and they could be a great help for you. Learn from them; ask them how they can support you. Also ask if the support is going to cost you, because sometimes they will charge you a fee or a percentage of your commission to help you, and you want to know that in advance. At the same time, they may be doing events and trips where you can plug in and support them.

A lot of Real Estate companies do not have an International Division, and that is a great opportunity for you to develop one, to be a support for all the Real Estate Agents in your office and get a percentage of their sales for managing the International Division.

If you have a vision to open the International Division, making an agreement with your Broker is important so you can start building your local team. I found this very exciting. If you are serious about developing an international business, be creative, because if you have the support of your Broker plus a team working with you, the results will come faster and you want to be prepared to respond. Share your goals with your team and align with them. Let them be part of your vision.

Creating a Plan to Succeed

As you have seen in this book, I am a big believer in planning. It could be the difference between succeeding and failing.

Understanding Your Customer:

Once you understand your customer you will be prepared to establish a strategy for that specific customer. You want to know: Who he/she is, what he/she does for a living, what is important to him/her, who the decision-maker and the influencer are, who else is involved in making the decision, what he/she wants and what he/she needs, what he/she expects. Remember that every customer is different.

Marketing Plan:

In a marketing plan several things are important. These are the ones I consider the most important to put your attention on.

Budget—Creating a budget helps you plan how much money you can invest in your business. Not having a budget could be dangerous because you start spending money instead of investing it, or you might invest more money that you should, or even under-invest.

To create a budget if you are starting your business, find out how much money you are willing to invest, then decide which activities will fit into your budget and give you the results in sales. Even if you don't have budget limitations, create a plan of activities that you would like to develop this year, put a price on each, and you will know how much money you will spend to develop those. Make sure to allocate an amount for extras (collaterals) so you have a little bit of room for changes.

If you already have your business going, one way to refine the budget is using a percentage of your income to re-invest in your business. Usually if you are new in a market you need to invest more. Once people start working with you, you will receive referrals and that will lower your costs.

When you have a budget and a plan about where to invest your marketing money, you will be more comfortable every time you need to pay because you were already prepared.

Media to use—As I explained before, make a list of the media that make more sense for you and will give you better results in your market. Put a price next to each item, then decide the frequency that you want to use each one. From this, create a media plan that will help you visualize how your efforts are going to be distributed and, at the same time, will keep you within your budget.

One of the key things that I learned was that even though you want to have a well-balanced media plan, you need to put more effort at the beginning of your campaign in a specific market in order to create branding. You could have peaks on your yearly media plan depending on how seasonal your market is; for example, just before a vacation season, if the tendency is for potential customers to travel to the US for vacation.

One of the myths about using mass media is they will give you volume because they reach more people. But the truth is that those people may not be the ones you need to target. You will have a better outcome in terms of results vs. money invested when you use media that go directly to your target market.

Remember, the main goal of using mass media is to build your name so people start to recognize you and your brand. Your goal for using mass media should not be sales. Even though this kind of advertising reaches thousands of people, it is expensive, and if you do not get enough prospective buyers, the return on your investment will be low or zero.

Promotions—This is a great tool to use when you are promoting specific products to international customers. Let's say you are promoting a community that can be offered to international buyers as a second / vacation home, and while they are not using it they can rent it to tourists. You may talk to the developer and make an agreement that for a certain time he will give an incentive to your international customers. For example, "no closing cost" or "maintenance covered for one year" or "flooring included," etc. You can use this to get more customers interested in a specific product. Just make sure that you have the written approval of the developer to offer this or any other type of promotion related with the project. Also make sure that while your customer is signing the contract, the developer also gives the customer in writing the specifications of the promotion so at closing there won't be any misunderstandings.

Promotions should be specifically to generate immediate response and to convert prospects to buyers.

Events—The Real Estate business is a people business, so here is where you can truly make contacts that you can convert later to either sales or to business partners.

There are several different types of events. You will use some to connect, some to teach, and some to promote your business. Some events you have to pay as a sponsor if you are promoting your business with a booth or logo, in some you need to pay only for traveling and entry fees to assist, and then there are the ones you have to create yourself.

Before you schedule an event in your plan, think about what outcome you want, and what you need to do to make that happen. For example, if you are going as a sponsor to an event where you have a booth, you need to have a banner, brochures, business cards, and some giveaways. All of that needs to be considered in your plan because that will cost money. At the same time, if you plan to do your own event there are many other details you need to consider, like audiovisual support, someone who takes care of registrations, etc. Travel is part of the event cost. Make sure that when you plan an event you are considering everything you need to make it happen.

Action plan—Once you are clear on how much money you want to invest in your marketing, what media you want to use and what other things you want to do, make a list of action steps you'll take during the whole year and start putting dates for when you will be doing each one. I will explain more about action plans because I believe they are the core of your business and are what will give you the direction to get you where you want to go.

Creating an Action Plan

The action plan is a document where you consolidate all the activities you need and want to do to develop your business. This written plan will keep you focused for the whole year. It is your map to action.

I have seen many different ways to develop action plans, but I like to keep it simple. The main components of an action plan are the list of action steps, responsibility or support, and a date line. If you use software like Microsoft Project, you also have other options, like the cost of the activities, amount of hours you need to invest in each activity, etc. It is great software to use if you want to invest money in managing your projects. I have been using Project for a long time, but I am sure you can manage your action plan without software, if you are well organized.

List of Actions:

You need to have a Master list showing each activity/action you will take to get to your goals. Each activity/action has a separate list of actions that have to happen to complete the whole task.

Let's say that you are planning to have an event. You place on your master list the name of the event, then you outline an action plan for developing that event: invitations, food and beverages, audiovisuals, presentation. But it doesn't stop there. Next you break this out one more time and have a list of actions per each main item. For example, for the invitations you list things like Create design, send it out, register guests, confirm. You will be itemizing every detail that is needed to make things happen the way you want.

One tip I would like to mention here is that you want to prioritize your tasks so you make sure you cover the most important ones first. Just know that prioritizing will change in light of what is the most important thing to do at the moment. I want to be clear on this aspect because it is not always the most important task of the year's preparation that has to be your number one priority. As you drill down to the basics, you'll see the whole picture in a different way. You'll notice how little things could make the difference in the whole project. To give you an example, most of the events that fail do so because the agent did not send the invitation on time. A little task in your project could make you fail or succeed, so put attention in every detail and do not leave anything out of the plan.

Another tip is that some actions need more itemization than others. Make sure that you go over the plan enough that you're sure you haven't forgotten anything that can affect the final result. This includes even the actions that you are not responsible to make happen but that are still important for the development of your plan. For example, the hotel needs to send you a quote if you are doing your event in such a venue. Another tip is including your team when you are creating the list for your action plan because you may be forgetting a step that is necessary to make the activity complete.

The more precise you are, the greater your chances to succeed, because you are taking care of what is required to get the results. When you have the whole picture mapped out, there is little room for error.

Responsibility and support:

Per each action you need to have someone who is responsible for that action. I know that right now, if you are working solo, you may think, "Well, there is not anyone else responsible but me." That is true in some ways, because you are responsible for the whole activity, but that does not mean that you are responsible for each action it takes to create that event or activity. In every activity, other people are involved — your Broker, an assistant, hotel personnel, the graphic designer, the media, if you are using them. In other words, every person involved with the activity is support for you in some way, even though at the end of the day you are the final person responsible.

The most important thing when you are creating an action plan and adding the names or roles of the people responsible is that you communicate with all of them. Let them know how important they are in your action plan. Once they feel important they will respond much better to your need to complete the task on time. You want to work with people who are committed to your plan, and the best way to get their commitment is sharing with them what is going on, what you want to accomplish, how you need things to happen, and why their part is so important. Always ask questions. For example, "This is what I need to happen. How do you think you can help me make this happen? What do you need from me so you can do your part the best way possible?" Their response will show their commitment to the task and to you, and they will sense that they have a mission and they will feel part of your team.

Remember always, when you are working with people, create rapport first if you want cooperation. Rapport will make you better in your communication and your listening. I have seen so many people who think that because they are paying they can talk down to others. Believe me, that does not work in the best interest of your results.

Date Line:

This one is critical. For everything that you do you must set a date line. No matter if you are the only one involved or there are more team players, committing to a date synchronizes you to what you plan to accomplish. In my experience, 90% of the tasks that do not have a date line are postponed to the point that they go to the list of "the forgotten." If you have an activity that is not important enough to have a date line, you may want to delete it from your list.

You can use the date line tool in two ways. One is to write beside the action step the final date that it needs to be completed. The other way, which is the one I use most of the time, is to place a start date and finish date on each action step. You will be able to accommodate each task in a way that looks balanced with your plan, and the action list will have a sense of flowing instead of rushing. If you are like me and you like rushing and you work better under pressure, that system may work if you are working solo. But I bet that in 80% of the cases there are more people involved than just yourself, and the majority of people do not play well under pressure.

Communicate with your team about the date lines. Just because you have set a date line does not mean that they can accomplish it, so always ask them, "How much time you will need to do this?" and "When do you think you will be able to finish this task?" Then you have a date line that is realistic, as well as their commitment to the date to finish the task.

If you have a time line that is tight you may say something like, "This part of the project needs to be finished by X date. What is the earliest you can finish this so we can get it on time?" If the dates do not fit, ask, "How can I help you or what do you need from me so you can finish no later than X date?"

Understanding how everything works and what needs to happen for people to do their job will give you more knowledge about the process, which leads to understanding from your support partners, which leads to more collaboration on their part.

Measure Your Plan

You need to measure your plan to know how you are doing, to find out what is working and what is not, to become more efficient in your choices for the next activities, which will increase the results in terms of sales.

The first thing that you need to do is look on your master plan and make sure you have described your goals in a way you can quantify and achieve. That could be sales, a number of contacts, or a certain number of business cards collected, etc. Let's go over an example: You are sponsoring an event attended by about 2000 guests. The event is going to last for three hours. If you say that you are going to make direct contact with 1000 people, that won't happen because you won't have the time to do that. Let's change your goal to make direct contact with 25 people, and in your booth you will collect about 100 business cards. Your next goal is to send out "Great to meet you!" emails to all of them and personally call 10 contacts per day.

Now you can measure what you did and the results, then adjust if necessary for the next event. Once you start doing this you will notice how much time and money you are investing in each activity and the results each one gives you. You will start choosing to do the activities that give you the better results and get rid of the ones that have been a waste of time and money.

Measure your plan at least every three months to get a better picture of the results of the activities in the short- and mid-term. When you do that you will be clear on what is working and what is not. Be flexible enough to improve something but also change some others and adjust your plan, incorporating new things. The key is that the plan works for you, not you for the plan.

Measuring a plan is something you need to do on a constant basis because at the end of the day you want to put your efforts in the right place.

How to Start Your Plan

Understanding International Marketing:

Each country has different laws and regulations about the use of advertising for different products. If you want to advertise in a magazine or newspaper in some countries, you need to do it through a local Real Estate Agent. In some countries you can't promote any price in US dollars. You have to use the local currency if you are advertising pricing. On the other hand, you have to be very clear that they must pay in US dollars so there is no misleading message.

Make sure you understand what you can and can't do when using the media, and when you do any type of promotion. In one country where I was working, I learned that if you launch a promotion where you are giving away any type of prize with a raffle, first you must tell the authorities what you are going to do so they approve it, and the day you are going to do the raffle someone from the government needs to be present as a witness. They also need to notarize the results. Your failure to do this could generate a fine and some other legal problems. Imagine creating a huge campaign and, after the message is out, you receive a call telling you that what you are doing is illegal and you need to stop it immediately, and by the way, you have to pay the fine!

The best way to get it right is to hire local experts who will take care of those details and let you know what you can or can't do.

Finding Local Support in Your Target Market:

You would like to have a group of experts that will be part of your support team to develop the activities you have planned for that specific market. Make sure the support team is in that country; you will need their knowledge to get better results.

In the next few lines I am going to talk about the professionals who are the most common to use. I will explain a little bit about what they do, how they usually charge for their services, and how to get the most out of it. Just remember that each country and each deal is different so you may find varying scenarios but these are the most common I have found.

Some of the professionals you would consider hiring are:

PR person / company— A PR, or Public Relations, person lobbies for you. That will open doors and also create branding. A PR person could be in charge of connecting you with the right people at institutional levels, getting interviews at the different media, organizing press conferences. Usually they charge either by the hour or by the project. I always prefer by the project because you do not have a way to control how many hours they invest.

They usually charge an honorarium for their job and if they are required to contract any service — say they are organizing a press conference for you — they charge you for getting the press together. They also charge, depending on the country, around 10% to 20% of the venue rental cost, as well as the cost of catering for coffee breaks and for AV rentals.

To get the best from them, make sure you are clear about what your goals are and their commitment to the results. About ten years ago I hired a PR company to take care of a press conference. They told me that they would get about twenty reporters from different media, but only about five showed up. The event cost a lot of money, and they did not take responsibility for their inefficiency. That was a costly lesson, but since then I request a minimum performance and I commit my payment to that. Some professionals won't accept that, and if that happens you need to choose whether you want to take a risk in working with them. If they are well known and have a proven record, you may want to take the chance. If you are not sure or they are new, my recommendation is to make sure that in some way they commit to the results of their job, and you have some written guarantee that if their job is not completed they are paid a lesser fee.

Advertising agency— An advertising agency will help you research the best media for your product. They will get you the pricing and suggest the frequency in light of what you want to achieve. Also, an advertising agency designs the artwork using the right words and images to reach that specific market. They could be a great support for developing your whole campaign, including any type of material that goes with the advertising.

They can also develop events for you, but my experience is that because agencies usually have to hire a freelancer or another company to do this, you pay more than if you go directly to an events organizer.

Advertising agencies usually have different types of charges. For creating the design and artwork, they get paid by the hour or a fixed fee. To negotiate for and buy the media spaces, they get a commission either from the media or they collect from you if you ask to pay the media directly. For the events or anything they have to hire from outside their office, they charge a percentage, usually between 5% and 20%. Some charge per project, but that is not usually the way it works.

The way to get the best from them is to interview them first and ask them in detail how they can support you. Ask about the way they charge, then decide what you want to use them for. You want to make sure you are not paying for things that you've already figured out or already have support for. If you have contact with the media and you are negotiating pricing directly with them, you don't need to pay the advertising agency to do that. If you have artwork you may want them to simply adapt it to the market instead of hiring them to create a new concept from scratch.

Advertising agencies can be expensive. You might also interview small advertising and marketing agencies, because you may find great people starting their own firms and they turn out to be the most successful. For a fraction of the price you may get the same results or even better ones. There are tons of agencies; just make sure you choose the one that delivers what you need and gives you good service, considering that you are not in the country.

Event Company / manager—Having an event manager will save you time and headaches. An event manager will take care of the logistics of an event that, for some, sound really easy but can turn into a nightmare if the hotel gives you the wrong room, or the room is not ready when people start arriving, or the menu that you request is not there at the coffee break, or they put the AV equipment in a different room, or the lunch that you receive is totally not what you ordered. In other words, having someone taking care of the details while you are presenting or working with the customers is important because your job is not organizing events; your job is selling.

Usually the event organizer/manager charges a fee per event, and if they are also in charge of booking the room, choosing the food for the coffee breaks, and making sure you have AV, then they may charge between 5% and 20% for those services.

To get the most from them if you already know where you want to hold the event, you can take charge of making the reservation and details, and ask your event manager to supervise that everything is as you requested.

The event manager should also be in charge of the registration process at the door, and when the event is finished the manager needs to close it, get the invoice from the venue, review it, and make sure that everything is taken care of. Also, you will have material (brochures, markers, computer, etc.) that needs to be packed. In other words, the event manager is the first one to get there and the last one to leave.

How to Choose and Work with Local Support

Make sure that you interview at least three in the category you are looking for, and ask powerful questions. A lot of decisions are made in light of a company's or manager's experience in the market that you want to reach, but I believe in giving value to the rapport that you have with them. Honor that feeling you get – sometimes you don't know where it comes from – that tells you which group is the right one for you.

Agreements:

I always ask them to sign a confidentiality agreement and, depending on what they are doing for me, sometimes I request that they do not get another customer who is my direct competition. Also ask for a non-disclosure because even though they are not working with your competition, you don't want your strategies to be revealed.

They usually have their own contracts, so read them in detail and make sure that they specify some type of guarantee that if they do not deliver, you get a discount. Obviously each case is separate and you want to make sure that you are clear on what you need and expect. If your expectations are too high, they should tell you what they will do instead, and then it is your choice to decide if that is what you want to do or not. Remember, they are the experts in that market and country, and they may tell you that what you want is not be possible in the way you want it. If that is the case, ask them what you can realistically expect.

If you have the choice of paying per hour or per project, choose per project. You'll have a lower probability of getting a surprise in the middle or end of your project, with extra hours needed or added.

Take Action, Make It Happen

Making a plan is important but taking action is even more so. Nothing is going to happen if you don't take the necessary steps to bring your plan into reality.

What Is Stopping You from Starting Right Now?

Think for a moment about what is stopping you right now. Is this something that has happened to you before? I believe that if you are reading this book it is because you are taking action to get more knowledge. Now what? Now you get the opportunity to put into practice what you are learning here.

I can tell you that maybe 50% of the people who go to seminars or read books or get any type of training go back home and do nothing with it. For me that is a waste of time and resources. When I ask people, "What did you learn and what did you apply immediately?" most of the time they know what they learned but they have not turned this into action. When I ask, "Why haven't you taken action yet?" all I hear are a bunch of objections that they created and put between them and their goals as obstacles. And guess what? Those obstacles are the ones that keep them living in a comfort zone.

Now I want you to think about a moment when you were at a crossroads, when you were making a decision between taking action or staying the way you are. Remember why you thought it was better to stay the way you were. Then go to another moment of your life when you experienced the same decision-making crossroads – could be as simple as whether to go on a diet to lose some weight. Notice if those objections/obstacles are the same.

All of us run patterns; we do the same thing over and over again, unless we break it. Usually those who say, "I don't have the time, I am too busy" are always busy. Those who say, "I don't know what to do" say the same thing for most of their decisions. Realizing what it is that you say to yourself every day will be the first step in breaking that pattern.

At this point you may be saying, "This is not me because I do whatever I want, when I want. I just need to make a decision and I do it …." I wish I could say to skip this chapter because you don't need this, but the truth is that if that is what you are saying, it is also a pattern. To be honest with you, that is the pattern I run. I say that over and over again. I am not saying that patterns are either good or bad. The reality is that patterns are part of who we are, and those patterns can empower us or disempower us. That is what you need to watch: How that pattern is affecting you life, whether it is serving you or not. Understanding your patterns and being aware of them if you choose to use them in your favor will change the way you do things and will take you to places you maybe thought were not possible.

The obstacles that we create are there to "protect" ourselves from our own fears.

Fear of failure—Failing is part of the process, and behind most of the successful people are stories about failing. Guess what? Failing is not failing if you use it to get better.

Fear of being rejected—Get this: In sales you are going to be rejected many times. If you are a new agent you probably are going to be rejected 8 or 9 times out of 10! So what? Remember, this is a numbers game, so get over it and enjoy saying, "NEXT!!" and use those No's as practice time.

Fear of not being good enough—If you prepare yourself, know your job and are professional in what you do, then not being good enough is just a matter of perception. My questions are: Do you think *I'm not good enough* just about yourself, or do you imagine that others think you aren't good enough? If you think that way about yourself, make a list of reasons why. They are usually weaknesses you perceive about yourself. Next, write the actions that you are going to take to minimize those weaknesses or maybe transform them into virtues. As you write, you will become aware that most of the list is just perceptions, not truths.

For example, you may think that because you do not speak the language perfectly you are not good enough. Well, take a class and get better. If the fear is about not being good enough for your customers, ask them, "What did you like about my service and how can I do better next time?" The best way to do this is with a customer service survey. It will be great for you to see how people perceive you.

Fear of losing the customer—This is going to happen eventually. You will work with a customer for hours, maybe days, maybe months, and then the customer meets somebody else and in two hours closes the deal. Again, that is part of the sales game. If you cannot live with that, you either need to change the way you perceive it or change your career.

Take Control and Break Through

As I said before, the doers have the power, and everything starts when you take that fear and use it to serve you in a way that moves you toward your goal.

Ask yourself how important this goal is to you, and I am sure that if it is important enough you will do what it takes to make it happen. I have met agents who worked really hard and they did not have the results. What I notice is that they are either playing safe or letting the fear control them in a way that will show up and the customer notices it. People can't always see fear, but they can sense it.

I have a friend who is about 50 years old, and he was telling me that he was frustrated because he was getting in and out of different direct-selling businesses, and he quit because he believed that he was not good enough at working with people and selling. I asked him, "In what activity do you think you are great?" and he said that he is great at collecting money for charity. In other words, he is terrible at selling where he makes a profit, but he does great and achieves excellent results when he collects money for others. What came up is his relationship with money: He feels guilty and not good enough when he does it for himself, but he feels great when he sells the cause of a charity because the benefit goes to others.

If you relate to the story of my friend, how does this behavior show up in your professional life? And what are the consequences you are dealing with because of that? Now that you know, what you are going to do about it? Life is about choices, and you create results in light of the choices that you make.

Have you made the right choices in the past? If your answer is yes, great, but remember that life is constantly changing, so the choices you need to make now may be different. Make sure that the choices you make now will bear results that will take you where you want to go.

Some of you may be overwhelmed at this point. What has worked great for me is to drill down. Remember the saying "How do you eat an elephant? One piece at a time"? Use the same strategy now. You are reading this book and I am talking about what you can do to develop your international market, and now I am talking about taking action and about fears. And I am doing it because everything starts from you, and if you are in a "fear" place, all the strategies I am giving you won't work.

I was working with a Realtor® who is one of the most amazing people I know. He cares about everyone, is a great friend and great father ... and a terrible sales agent because when he gets to the point of closing the sale, he just freezes. He was so scared of people that I was amazed at how someone could show such polarity. It was like seeing two totally different people. He was very successful on the personal level; he was really unsuccessful on the professional level. Once he understood what he was doing and feeling on the personal level, we were able to take that step by step to the professional level, to the point that he is starting to be successful professionally too.

During all my years of going to seminars, what I see in common from all the successful trainers is that they give special attention to visualizing what you want. The book/movie "The Secret" is the best example of this. This movie explains in a simple way that you are the creator of your life, so design it the way that you want it and you will attract what you are going for. The key thing, though, is that if you do design your life on paper — for example, doing a treasure map or dream board — then put it on the wall and look at it every day. Just doing the exercise by itself is not going to work, but if you use that dream board to inspire you to do what it takes to have that dream life, then magic will happen. The dream board is going to act as the Why, and that will inspire you to move forward. Visualizing what you want is important, but then you need to visualize yourself taking action to make it happen. Even more important: Take physical action. Do something!

Get Yourself in the Right State of Mind

The state of mind that you are in most of the time is either going to help you move forward or hold you back. It will show in your actions, which translate into results. Let's say that Real Estate Agent George feels totally upset about the situation in the market, and he basically does not believe that anyone should be buying now, and if they do they will lose their money. Next, he gets a call from one of his customers in Mexico, who says that he is coming to the US and wants to spend two days with George to look for properties to invest in. George gets excited that he has a customer coming, so he searches for the best properties. When he meets with the customer, ready to show properties, the customer asks, "So, George, what do you think about the market? By the way, George, I am so excited to be buying in this moment because I think this is the right market for investors." Imagine what is going to happen with George. The way he thinks and feels about the market will, for sure, affect his answer and therefore his sales.

It is important to understand that there is a huge difference between an opinion and a state of mind. The opinion is something you believe. A state of mind is the way you feel right now (based on your thoughts and beliefs), and it's reflected in the way you talk and in the way you act. It affects everything around you in either a positive or negative way.

My mentor, Joe Williams, taught me that 20% of doing anything is about technique, and 80% is about your state of mind. That is why so many people do what the book says but do not get the results. Getting results is more than book-learning. What you are learning from a book is just 20%. You have to put the other 80% into becoming who you need to be so you get the results you are looking for.

I have been a believer in personal development because giving attention to all the areas of my life helps me be a whole person. I believe that if I am in the right place emotionally, physically, spiritually and professionally, I succeed as a whole, and success will become a way of living. I have being listening and learning from many mentors and always go for getting the best from them, not only giving 100% of my attention to what I am hearing, but also taking at least two to five things and putting them into immediate action.

The Power of Having a Mentor/Coach

A coach is someone who sees outside the picture and is there to ask the right questions, to show you possibilities that you did not see before, to challenge you to step up and do what needs to be done to have the results you want. A coach acts as an accountability partner and can become an essential part of your business and success. If you do not have a coach, get one now, someone who helps you achieve what you need to in this moment of your life. There are several types of coaches, and you need to find the one that is right for you. You could even have more than one coach – one who helps you now for something specific, and one who has a different specialty. Six months after I got my Real Estate coach I changed coaches because I had gotten where I needed to with the first one, and I needed someone with different skills to help me move even farther forward.

A mentor is someone with more experience than you, a role model, a teacher, someone who is already where you want to go, someone who walks the talk and is willing to share with you and others what he/she got there – the good, the bad, and the ugly of his/her experiences – and would like everyone to learn to be better than they are. You can have several mentors or coaches at the same time, and your mentors could be your parents, a friend, a colleague, or even trainers and speakers who are experts on what you want to develop.

My coach when I was 22 years old taught me about the concept of having a "Board of Directors." This means that you have a group of people in your life to whom you go when you have a challenge, or maybe an important decision to make. You talk to them and they will give you different perspectives based on their own experiences. I am sure you have those special people you seek out when you need to make a decision. What if you start using this concept in a more conscious way and you took the best from having your very own Board of Directors?

As I said before, accountability is one of the most critical reasons for having a coach, and if you don't want to have a coach just talk to everyone around you and tell them what you are planning to do. It is funny because where I come from, a lot of people are superstitious. They advise, "Don't say what you are going to do before you do it because if you say it, it won't happen." They keep it secret and most of the time it doesn't happen anyway. For me it has worked much better the other way around. When I want something to happen I go and tell everyone so I create accountability partners. I can be sure that if I share with a friend that I am going to do something, the next time we meet this friend will ask me, "So how are you doing with X?" If you are planning to develop your international business, start telling everyone and you won't be able to hide it.

Make sure you keep yourself to the highest standards, as that is the only way to achieve success. If you are comfortable with less than that and you want just stay where you are, fine; just be sure it's not a decision you will regret. The best way to maintain your high standards is being with people who live by high standards.

Making it happen is about you, what you think, how you behave, and what you do. You are 100% responsible for what happens in your life; and, of course, what happens after you finish this book. And also for what happens if you don't finish it.

CHAPTER 6
RESOURCES FOR DEVELOPING YOUR INTERNATIONAL BUSINESS

Hire a Coach

In Chapter 5 I explained why I believe it is important to have a coach and the benefits one will bring to your life. Now I would like to go over some distinctions that will help you pick the best coach for you.

How to Choose the Right One for You:

There are thousands of coaches in the US, for almost every kind of business. Deciding which is the best for you basically comes down to the one you feel most confident in. In other words, while there are a few things you need to consider when hiring a coach, the most important is that you have rapport with him/her. This person is going to support you to develop your career, and to do that they will tap in to professional as well as personal issues that may be holding you back.

Experience in the field you want to develop is important, though I have seen lots of successful coaches who aren't. If I were looking for a coach, I would choose one who has done in the past what I want to do now. Why re-invent the wheel when somebody else already learned from the experience?

For me, it has to be someone I admire and respect as a professional. Then I will value even more what I am receiving from him/her. But the most important thing for me is that this person "walks the talk."

Affording a Coach:

Evaluate the cost of having a coach vs. how much business you will gain as a result of what you learn. I.e., cost vs. value. Having a coach is an investment, and positive results show up as increased sales, more customers, and a greater closing rate. If the results are not what you expected, you have to evaluate why. Are you not being coached efficiently? Have you not been coachable? Is there not enough rapport between you and your coach? If so, you may want to change coaches.

What to Expect:

A coach helps you see things you are not seeing yourself, and will teach you tools to increase your profitability. The main thing about having a coach is that you create accountability for keeping yourself on track and sticking to your plan, for getting back on track, or even renegotiating your plan.

A coach also has the advantage of seeing what you are experiencing from the outside. With his/her experience, they will support you to look for better ways to do things. At the same time they are giving you feedback. Someone asking the right questions helps you become the best at developing your business.

Types of coaches:

Many coaches have specialties. They focus on various areas and use different techniques. I like those who make sure you are supported as a whole person in your professional and personal life, who work with you on your state of mind, fears, and other challenges that may be holding you back. Usually if a sales agent is not getting results, something is going on at a personal, spiritual or mental level. Maybe the agent is in the middle of a divorce, or has a huge fear of rejection, or does not believe in himself. A good coach should be prepared to address those types of situations and be capable of supporting the sales agent in anything that could affect his performance.

Attending Trainings

Defining Your Career Plan:

Do you know your expectations for the future of your career? Do you know how you are going to get there? Do you know what you need to learn in order to get there? These are basic questions to answer if you are serious about developing this career. Your answers will tell you how much commitment you have for this business. International Real Estate is hard work, which does not mean it's difficult. In International Real Estate if you do the right thing and have consistency and knowledge, you could be very successful, but it requires a lot of commitment to make it a career.

Before you can move forward, you need to know where you are right now, and where you want to be. That will show you the gap between now and the future.

The next step is laying out the action plan to take you where you want to go.

One tool that I use is S-W-O-T, which analyzes your Strengths, Weaknesses, Opportunities and Threats.

Strengths—These are your strengths as a professional: What you do different that sets you apart from your competition; those things in which you are an expert; and what you do that is outstanding (not average, but better than the competition).

Weaknesses—These are things you don't do very well, things you need to improve, to delegate to others, or not do much of. This could include those things that your competitors do well and you do not.

Opportunities—These are from the market, from the outside in. Opportunities are the same for everyone, you and your competitors.

Threats—What threats will or could affect your competitors' business and yours?

Doing this analysis will give you a better picture of you and your career. You'll find out in which areas you need more development and which areas you are strong. In the past, the tendency was to take the weaknesses and work on them until they stopped being weaknesses. However, people spent too much effort on areas of slow growth. Now the tendency is toward taking the strengths and working with those even more.

Finding the Best Training for You:

Because there are several trainings out there for the different aspects of your business, choosing the right one might be challenging. Before you get into the first one you find, do a little bit of research.

Your local Board of Realtors® is the best place to start because they have great people doing trainings and sharing their experiences at a fraction of the price. Allocating a budget for trainings is a smart thing to do.

Training takes time. Lay out a schedule and a goal of how many hours a month you will spend at trainings. When I started doing Real Estate in the US, I had a goal to take two trainings per month, and that kept me on track for creating what I wanted to accomplish.

Remember that a key thing is balance. If you get too much training and do not start applying what you have learned, it won't help. You need to put it into immediate practice.

Put into Action What You Learn:

One of the most common problems is that people go to seminars and get overwhelmed with tons of new tools and information. They don't know where to start and don't do anything with what they learned.

I ask participants who attend my trainings or talks to make two columns on a sheet of paper. One is for "great ideas" and the other one is a "to-do list." I ask them to write things down while I am talking so they don't lose any thoughts. It is great to have two different categories—"great ideas" and "to-do list"— because the fact that you heard a great idea does not mean that you have to do it now, or need to take it to action in the short term. You may take that great idea and use it a year later. While you are listening, you are writing ideas, but you do not create timelines until you finish and decide which you will do now. Commit to only those activities which will support your business right now.

At the end of the event, I ask the participants to check the three greatest ideas they got from the event, then I ask them to place each one in the to-do list with at least the first action and date line. Committing to certain actions before you leave the training or before you finish this book will give you encouragement and leverage to start immediately. If you take this strategy to every event you attend, you will leave each one with a plan.

Another way to become an expert in what you are doing is by teaching, so I encourage you to learn and then teach it to somebody else. Go back to your office and take one or maybe a few of your colleagues and teach them what you just learned. That will make you go over the material again, and at the same time create accountability partners at your office because they will watch and learn from you.

Having accountability partners is a great way to keep the commitments that you make at the trainings. If the speaker or trainer does not ask you to find an accountability partner, I encourage you to do it yourself. Just pick someone you met at the training or someone you already know who is committed to the results and ask him/her to be your accountability partner. Make sure to share what you are committed to do and by when, and then commit to follow up with each other once a week about how things are going and the progress you have made. The great thing about having accountability partners who have been at the event is that they have the same info you do. It's especially helpful if you missed or misunderstood something, or just did not get it.

Knowing vs. Doing:

Doing is more important than knowing. Doing is what is going to bring you results, and results equal money. A balanced training schedule will support you in your action plan.

When will you know enough to start doing? That is one of the questions that agents ask and I always say, "You need constant training. As the market changes, new things come and you need to be updated. But do not wait until you think you know enough because that day will never come."

I had a sales agent who got her license and was under the belief that she needed to be trained before she could have contact with customers. She was in this state for about three months, going to trainings almost every week. Then, in a one-on-one coaching session, I asked how she was applying what she had learned. She realized that she didn't remember most of the things, even though she had written them down, because she had not used them.

I encourage you to create a training schedule that allows you enough time between events to process and start practicing what you learn immediately. You will be able to grow in more consistent and strong ways.

Training Resources:

The best way to have access to great trainings in an affordable way is to look first at the trainings that come from the National Association of Realtors®, Real Estate associations, and your local board. Their people are trained and put together different programs. To learn more about their programs, go to www. realtor.org and look for the International section. You will see all the trainings and certifications they offer.

If you are looking for training outside the NAR®, make sure that the trainer is an expert in their field.

Strategic Liaisons

Creating Long-term Relationships:

Your main goal when you start relationships is to develop and maintain trust with your business partners. Stephen M. R. Covey, the son of Stephen Covey, wrote a great book called "The Speed of Trust" that I believe every business person should read.

Real Estate Agents who have the most success are customer service-oriented, so create a plan for pre-sale and post-sale services. If you want to know more about customer service, look for books on how the big companies are doing it and apply to your business the simple ideas that have made them succeed. A book that I like very much is "Inside the Magic Kingdom: Seven Keys to Disney's Success," by Tom Connellan.

Align with your partner if you want to be successful, and that has to be with communication and leadership skills. Make sure that you express to your liaisons what you expect from them from the beginning. Make the customer your first priority because you are creating liaisons to add value and better serve them. As Real Estate Agents, it is important to have a high-quality group of professionals in different areas so you can give a list to your customers and they can choose the best option for them. At the same time, follow up with your customers to make sure that the service they are receiving is on a high standard. The moment that you see that a liaison is not giving good service is the time to get someone else.

Remember, your international customer trusts you. Often you are the first face he sees and the first person he has contact with when he comes to do Real Estate here.

Lawyers:

Before you refer your customers to lawyers, do your research. Are they experts in Real Estate for International Customers? Do they speak the language of your customer? When you need to negotiate or explain a contract, translators are not reliable because one incorrectly translated word can change the whole meaning of a sentence. Use translators only if that is the only resource available. Most lawyers charge by the hour. Try to negotiate your customer's first consultation for free.

Additionally, check if the lawyer has had any major complaints lodged with the local legal agencies.

Accountants:

Having an accountant for an international customer is a must because they will need to file taxes in the US and in their country. Be sure that the accountant is knowledgeable about the applicable tax laws. The accountant needs to speak the language of the customer.

Not all accountants are experts in Real Estate. Based on the type of property that your customer has, and the type of structure he needs to create in order to own the properties and manage his real estate business, I recommend using an accountant who is an expert in Real Estate for International Customers.

Accountants also charge by the hour. Most of the time there is an initial consultation, and then usually they charge a flat fee for preparing and filing the taxes. You can also request that your referrals get one free consultation as part of the accountant's service.

Mortgage Brokers:

Your customers should work with mortgage brokers who have experience with International Buyers, because International Customers may qualify for different types of mortgages and programs with different rates and time schedules. Not all banks work with International Buyers because some information that an International Buyer gives to the bank cannot be verified like we do in the US with a Social Security number. Some banks do not want to risk lending money to an International Buyer without being sure that he qualifies to pay the mortgage. Make sure that the mortgage broker has contacts with those banks offering the best programs to International Buyers.

Even though an expert is going to process the mortgage for your customers, you need to know what they will be asked for as International Buyers. They will be required to have a US Tourist Visa in order to be approved by the bank. If your customer does not have one, he may be unable to close. Understand also that requirements change with time. If you are selling properties that are going to close in a year or more, be very clear that things could change. What banks are requesting today may be different later.

A few years ago banks were asking qualifying Foreign Nationals to put down 20%. Later that changed to 25% to 30%. You need to be informed so you can inform your customer. At the same time, be very clear about the changes they may face so they will be prepared and you reduce the surprise factor.

Other Resources:

Customers may need other resources, like a handyman, home insurance company, moving company, title company, etc. Be prepared to provide a list of professionals to your International Customer. Some Real Estate Agents include such a list in a Buyer or Seller package. The most important thing is to be prepared so you have the information handy when the customer asks for it.

On the other hand, remember that your customer may not know what he needs to ask for, so it's up to you to explain how important it is for him/her to work with a professional and how they will support him in the process.

CHAPTER 7
BECOMING AN INTERNATIONAL PRO

Transform Your Obstacles/Objections into Your Biggest Strengths

In Chapter 5, I went over some of the objections we tell ourselves, which become the obstacles that hold us back from developing our business successfully. Once you recognize what is holding you back, you have the opportunity to transform those objections into some of your biggest strengths.

Some of this section will sound a little bit repetitive, but these few pages are a review of key things that are a must for you to master.

Your Primary Language:

As a Spanish-speaking person, believe me when I tell that even today the fact that I do not speak 100% perfect English holds me back sometimes. But also I realize that speaking two languages gives me a competitive advantage when I sell my services. Even though you do not speak a language 100% perfectly, you are ahead of your competition because most of the sales agents are not bi-lingual. If you speak a language that may not be common in the US, that gives you an even bigger opportunity because you can support and team up with other local Realtors® who receive business from countries where that language is spoken.

I met a Realtor® who speaks Russian. She has been offering her services to Realtors® and Real Estate Agents. Most of the time she helps them work with their customers who speak Russian. For her, this has been a huge opportunity because she is working with other Real Estate Agents and getting a percentage of the deal just because she speaks the language and understands the culture.

If you are getting customers from countries that speak a different language than you do, you may want to team up with someone who speaks their language and understands their culture. Your rate of closing will go higher when you have someone who can communicate efficiently with the customers. Another way to do it if you don't have a Real Estate Agent in your area who can support you is to hire a translator, but I believe that is not that as efficient as having someone with language and Real Estate skills working with you.

When choosing a market to develop, get into ones where either you know the language or you have someone on your team who can support you with that.

Build a Network:

I have taken some of my experience in the corporate world to my Real Estate world, and one of the things I have noticed is that not many agents team up. Based on my conversations with several Real Estate Agents, I believe that they don't team up because they fear losing customers if they work with somebody else.

Teaming up could be the key to your rapid growth and success in this business. Most of the successful Real Estate sales agents have teams, so working with a team could make a positive difference in your business.

Build a network that will support you, help you grow consistently, and give you credibility in the market you are developing. Be selective in choosing your local peer group for that market. Remember, people may do not know you there, but they may know the people you are relating with. Depending on who they are, that can help you or hurt you, so make sure that you team up with people you are proud to be associated with.

Building a network takes time and effort but if you do it right you will create a strong base for your business that supports you for the long term.

Become the Expert in Your Target Market:

Customers like to work with agents who know what they are doing. I know this could be a learning process, but it is totally worth it so take the time you need if you are really serious about this business.

The best way to learn is to practice. As I said before, you will learn lots by doing and evaluating your results.

And remember, always learn from the best—they already walk that path. You want to be surrounded by professionals who are getting the results you want because that will make you stretch and become better and better. You have to reach for higher standards to be motivated and inspired to do more as you learn.

Be an Expert at Overcoming Your Own Objections:

Prepare, prepare, prepare. This is a must if you want to minimize what is holding you back. Why? Just think about this: If you prepare, the chances of failure get lower. Preparation is not only learning through books and trainings. When I say *Prepare*, learning and training have to be combined with practice.

It is amazing the way our minds work, so attend to your state of mind. Work on being in a resourceful state that will support you and your business. Being in a state of fear won't serve you and might keep you from developing your international business. Believing in yourself empowers you. I believe that we create the reality we live. If you firmly believe that something is an obstacle, it is, but you have the power to transform your beliefs.

The best way to overcome your objections is to do what you need to do, no matter what. Do not allow the fact that you have objections to get in your way. I can tell you from my own experience that you can reach any level of success you decide to. You just need to make the decision and do it. Things won't come to you just because you are sitting there being a nice person. Things come to you because you create the opportunity for them to come, through preparation and action. Remember the law of action-reaction: Every reaction is a result of an action. What are you going to create that will bring you what you want? Once you know that, do it.

Teaming Up for Success

The best way to tame your objections/obstacles and get going on your action steps is to create a team of people who support you in different ways. As you read before, I am a big believer in building high-performance teams.

Internationally:

Once you know your goals and what it takes to get you there, make a list of all the support you need and start looking for the right people and companies to fill your needs. Make sure that you interview them before choosing the one for you.

When you build your team, know what you can and can't do, both in this country and your target market. You want to get the most out of your activities without creating any problems. Become a master at networking because there is no limit to the things you can achieve when you have the right people guiding your way.

The key to maintaining those relationships you create is delivering what you committed to. It's best to have everything in writing; at the same time, there are lots of things you will talk about and you may forget or maybe won't feel the need to put those in writing. However, it is a must to do what you committed to if you want to have credibility and build long-term relationships.

Locally:

Invest in your growth on an ongoing basis. Team up with people who are aligned with you and your goals, or whose goals you can align with. Remember that your time is money, so every minute that you invest in your growth you have to get a return on your investment that will make it worth your time. If you hire a coach, they will be a key member of your team, helping you to be centered and focused.

Having an assistant could also be one of your best investments. I found this out myself in the middle of handling paperwork. I believed I was wasting my time on administrative stuff that anyone could handle, but I also knew that paperwork was important. The problem was that I wasn't doing it as efficiently as a good assistant could. Besides, I wanted to take care of what I do the best:

sales. At first I still didn't hire an assistant because I wanted to keep all the money for me. But when I evaluated how much non-selling work I had to do, I decided to hire one. That's when I realized all the work hours that the assistant took away from me, and all the NEW free time I now had to contact more people and sell. My business doubled that year.

If you have as part of your team a group of Real Estate Agents who are willing to work with you, learn from you, and be coached by you, you will be able to expand even more. Look for people who have strengths that you do not have so they complement you. On the other hand you want to limit the number of people on your team. What that "right" number is depends on what you want.

If you are developing an office your number could be different than if you are developing a small team to work with you directly. Before you decide how many people to have on your team, know what you want to accomplish. You can also start with a small team and grow based on your needs. The team must support you instead of control you. If you start with a big group that you need to train and take care of, you won't have the freedom to work on your own business. Your priority will be to serve your team because they will leave if you don't support them and they do not make money. You really want to give it some thought, to create a team that will help and support your business goals. It is not about how big is your team; it is about how efficient it is.

The external support people who do your marketing, website, etc., are also part of your team, even though they are freelancers or hired by the project.

Other Key People on Your Team:

Make a list of all the support professionals your customers may need, from lawyers, accountants, mortgage brokers, and also handymen, inspectors, etc. Create a directory listing three persons for each category. Make sure to follow up with your customers about the services they received from the person(s) they chose, and keep on the list only the ones who are doing a great job for your customers.

Build and Protect Your Business

When you are building your international business you are working with different cultures and adapting in some way to how they do business. At the same time they will be learning from you how to do business in your market. I recommend taking these basic steps so your business is protected.

International Agreements with Affiliates:

When working with international agents, keep everything in writing. Even when you have a conversation, at the end write an email based on your notes to make sure you did not misunderstand anything and that your points were understood. To avoid misunderstanding, I usually close the email something like this: "Please let me know via return email if I forgot to add anything or if something that I wrote is not what we agreed so I can make the changes on this document. If I do not receive any comments from you regarding this matter in the next two days, I will understand that the information here is correct." I add, "Please confirm that you have received this email." If they do not respond within 24 hours, I send it again and in the Subject line I add: "2nd SENDING" and" YES!!!" in capital letters. This never fails.

Open a file on your computer where you save all the documents, emails or anything that pertains to that relationship. Be sure to back up your computer onto a hard drive. You can use Outlook or other contact manager software to keep a record of the conversations, follow-ups and pendings.

Make sure you are clear as to what you expect. Listen when the other party tells you what they expect. Then you both can be on the same page. Communication is a basic skill that you need to develop whenever you're doing business, but when you are doing business internationally it is even more important that you develop it to the highest level. The best way to open the communication channels is to ask questions and listen to the responses. Understand where they are coming from and make sure that if you do not agree with them that you explain your point with respect and without making the other party wrong.

When there is a conflict in the relationship with your international liaisons, the first thing you want to do is have a conversation and look for a solution together. If that is not possible, find a mediator, someone from the outside who does not have an interest in the deal. I highly recommend that you consider doing the

TRC certification from ICREA, because they have a system already in place where all the members of the associations that are part of ICREA anywhere in the world have access to their mediation services for a fee.

Agreements with Customers:

Make sure that you are clear in your communications from the very first meeting. Remember that this may be their first experience buying in your market, so you want to make sure that the process is understood. Explain the process in detail, even the basic stuff. You never know how something that seems to be a small detail to you can become a problem for the customer. If you take the time to know and understand how the process works in their country, you will be able to make the distinctions between how it's done in their country and the US.

After an experience of showing properties to a customer and then knowing that he went to the same property by himself to buy directly or with another agent, I now ask them to sign a Buyer's Agreement before I show them property. I explain the benefits of becoming my customer under such an agreement. Sometimes they like having someone representing them; sometimes they just want you to work with them without an agreement. It is then your choice if you want to work with the customer or not.

Another option when the customer does not feel comfortable signing a Buyer's Agreement is to use a Buyer's Agreement for each property that you show him/her. If you want to learn how to work with and represent buyers, I recommend that you take the ABR® certification (Accredited Buyer Representative certification) with NAR® so you will learn techniques to get the customers to work with you, and how to protect your work. What I learned in this course helped me protect my commissions.

Again, the secret of good relationships is communication, so I recommend that you also use with your customers what I just talked about using with your liaisons / partners. Remember to keep a record of everything.

I believe that the best way to avoid problems is to do your job and commit to the results your customer is expecting. Once your customer sees your commitment to him, he will like working with you and won't feel the need to find somebody else. Remember, your job is not complete until it is 100% done. This means that your job is not to find a property; your job is to support the customer all the way until he closes and receives the property. Being by the customer's side during the whole process will make a huge difference in his buying or selling experience.

Challenges:

One of the biggest challenges that International Real Estate Agents face is that the liaison made contact with other local Real Estate Agents, and after learning the business they felt free to go with another agent and request bigger referrals fees. If you want to avoid this, make sure that you are professional in the way you work. Remember, this is a relationship business, and people will continue working with you if they believe you are the right person to work with.

On the other hand, even though you already have an agreement with your liaison, make it clear that you pay referral commissions after the customer closes the deal, and that sometimes the referral is going to be higher and sometimes it is going to be lower. This way, your liaison won't think that you're being unfair, and he will have the opportunity to renegotiate the referral with you before he goes to somebody else if he thinks that he deserves a higher referral fee.

With customers, another big challenge is that they are shopping around. Most countries do not have something like MLS, so international customers believe that they need to work with ten different Real Estate Agents before they can find what they are looking for. Explaining how the MLS serves the Real Estate professional in the US will help you keep the customer. Just remember that the customer has the right to work with whomever they want. They may have the intention to work with you, then go to somebody else because they did not like your service, or because they did not like what you showed them, or just because another Real Estate Agent happens to be in the right place at the right time. The customer has the right to do that. The way to keep your customer is by giving a high standard of service, to exceed their expectations and to build a strong relationship so they will stay with you and also refer other potential customers. People do business with people they like, honor and respect.

The Sales Cycle

Understanding the sales cycle of the Real Estate business will save you time and money. Instead of worrying about what's going on that you are not seeing results, you will be focused on creating more opportunities for your business.

Time Is Your Friend:

If you have seen me speak, I am sure that you heard me say, "I believe that you either use the time in your favor or against you." Be smart and let time be your friend. This business requires time. It is not a business where you can place an ad in a magazine and suddenly you are inundated with calls. This is a business where you need to create your reputation and build your image as an expert in your market while investing in activities that give you access to your target market.

There is always a gap of time between when you contact the customer and the customer closes the deal. The first three months are probably the most challenging. You start contacting customers, and you start seeing results. But some of the activities you have done will take longer to give results. People call when they are ready to. I received a response to an email sent three months earlier, and guess what—he bought a property from me. If you don't see immediate results in an activity, do not stop, especially if it's been proven by others that this activity works. At one point the business will start to pop. I like to make the analogy with popcorn, because the effect is similar, it just takes a bit longer. Before you know it you be adding businesses to your pipeline and having more results in terms of higher numbers on a monthly basis.

It took me thirty days to get my first deal. I was on the phone calling everyone I knew, asking for referrals and then calling those referrals for more referrals. I spent hours and hours prospecting until I had my first customer and closed a deal. A few months later, I started to receive calls and emails from people I had contacted months earlier. They were ready to start looking or knew someone interested in buying, and little by little I built my business.

On the other hand I also know what happened with some of the Realtors® I have met either working with me or in my seminars. What I have seen is that some people do not have consistency. They "tried" and then got tired of not seeing results and quit. When I asked them what they did, most of them did not do what is needed to build a business.

I want to be very clear with you—this is a business like any other business. If you want to make money, you have to work, invest time, money and energy getting knowledge so you are able and ready to compete in one of the most competitive environments in the sales world. You need to "do" consistently to get results, and "doing" includes treating this business like the business it is. You need to prospect, do presentations, be with your customers during the entire process and follow-up, and ask for more business and referrals.

I believe that you can create the right moment for you to be in this business. As I said before, there is no good or bad market. This is a business in constant fluctuation—sometimes more demands than offers, sometimes more offers than demands. It is a cycle, and time will show you how its cycles come and go. You may be just right there, about to start exploding your business, and if you decide to quit you may be losing the results of three to six months of work. The key is to be consistent.

Advertising and Marketing Efforts:

In many cases, the activities give you some sort of immediate response, if nothing more than a contact back. Let's say you have an event. The immediate response is that the participants call you back or give you the opportunity to meet with them. Do not, however, expect to sell ten properties at an event, because that is not what happens.

When developers travel to do presentations, some people get the checkbook out and make a contract, or a letter of intent, because they are following their emotions. In Florida at the time that this book was written, we have a law that says that the buyer has fifteen days after signing a contact on a pre-construction property to cancel without penalty. I have seen agents coming back from a trade show with fifteen to twenty contracts, but at the end of the fifteen-day rescission period, only three to five stay and the rest cancel. At most events, you want to identify the people who are really interested. In some way pre-qualify them before you have a private meeting to go over the different options available.

As you increase your experience, you will be increasing your closing rate. You may start with an average of closing 10% of the time, and eventually get to a closing rate of 90%. If you are lower than that, you need to work on developing your skills. To do that requires assessing your strengths and weaknesses, as shown in Chapter 6.

Events:

At events, the sales cycle often is faster than in other types of activities. Usually you will have immediate response from a big percentage of the people who are willing to buy. When I say "immediate response" I mean up to ninety days, and long-term responses could be between one and three years.

You also will have surprises. For example, two years after an event, someone may contact you to say that now is when they are ready to buy. In my opinion that is really great because if someone who met you two years ago is calling you now, it is because you made an impact on them and he/she is looking forward to working with you.

Working with Customers:

It is important to understand that the customer is going to make their decision when they are ready. Do not push the customer. They will feel the pressure, and you will lose them sooner or later. Customers can sense when you just want a commission and when you really care for them. I have a friend who says that the customers can smell "the commission breath." Remember that selling is about serving the customer, so make the process about the customer instead of yourself, your goals and your commissions.

Working with a customer starts from the moment you are in front of him/her until the deal is closed and you do your follow-up. Whenever you meet anyone, build that relationship and do not worry about the time line. There is not an exact time or formula how it should be. What you need to be worry about is whether the customer is comfortable working with you.

Each customer is different. Start understanding what is behind your customers' words to really get how you can serve them in the best way possible. With some customers, the best way may be to tell them that they are not ready to buy if you see that they cannot afford the financial stress of the purchase they want to

97

make. I know some of you right now are thinking, "They are the ones to decide if they invest or not." I have seen people wanting to buy properties just to fit in socially. They were using all of their saving to go to closing. That is an example of one of those moments where you want to show your customers the numbers and make sure that they are making a smart choice for them, rather than one that will make them struggle financially. Use the help of a mortgage broker if you need to. They will give the customers the numbers and show what they could do with the money that they want to dedicate to their investment.

Asking the right questions and listening to the customers' answers will make you more assertive and confident, and success will follow that.

CHAPTER 8
CUSTOMER SERVICE FOR INTERNATIONAL CUSTOMERS

Everything is about the experience, so what experience are you creating for your customers? International customers have different needs than locals expect or require, and delivering on them will make your customers come back for more as well as refer more business to you. I "grew up" professionally in corporations that work under the belief that you need to exceed a customer's expectations.

Maintaining Your Relationship with International Customers

If you've read this far, you know that building relationships will give you more business than advertising, events, or any other type of activities you are planning. Creating a business relationship is easy; what is hard is maintaining it.

When I say to build relationships with your customers, I am not saying that you have to become his/her best friend. No. The more you work with them, the more your customer feels confident in you, relies on you to be on top of every detail and taking them by the hand to show them the path.

But if you want to build a long-term relationship you need to do more than that. You need to create services that add value to your customers' experience, save them time and money, and help them be more efficient.

To do this, find out what their values are and direct them to services supporting that. Let's say that your customer values quality time with their kids. Create a list of places where they can take their kids for fun. You can even support them by helping them make reservations. As simple as this may sound, it makes a difference.

One of my first experiences working in Real Estate in the US was with a customer who mentioned while we were looking at properties that she needed to get some blue jeans for her daughter. When we finished, I took her to a very cool shop and she got the jeans. While I was waiting outside the store, I was thinking "What a waste of time!" A couple of years later she called me. She was traveling with her family, and they invited me to lunch. They had a list of things they wanted to do, and needed my help to know which places would be the best. I had the opportunity to meet her family, particularly her daughter. Based on what her mom told her, I was the one who knew where to go for the things she wanted to get. We spent lunch making a list of places, including addresses and directions. At the end of lunch the mother said, "Oh, by the way, when you will be available to go over some properties?" They put a contract on a property that week.

If you ask the right questions and invest time getting to know your customer, you will be able to create relationships for life. Remember that you do not need to do it yourself. Find experts to team up with so you can do what you do best while they do what they do best.

I have to stress again how important it is to keep your customer informed about what is going on with their properties, with the market, and even with anything in which they are interested. I have a customer who loves boats, so every time we have a boat show I send him an email about it. I usually get an email back, saying, "Yes, I am coming."

Once a customer emailed me that when he saw my notice about a show, he got airline tickets, but now he could not find a hotel close to the event. He wanted my recommendation where to stay. I called a few hotels and found a room for him. It took maybe twenty minutes of my time, but I can assure you that he knows he can count on me when he comes to my city, so when he is ready to buy or sell he will contact me.

Here is the deal: Buying property is one of the most, if not *the* most, important investment that your customer is going to make in his/her life. For me this is a huge opportunity to help them do things right. This is about helping them achieve their goals and dreams. To do that, I listen to what they are saying and what they are not saying.

A perfect example of this is an interview I had with a couple. It was funny and at the same time alarming. He responded totally different than she did to every question I was asking. It was like a tennis match. They were not even on the same page. First I had to support them to get aligned so I could help each one get what they wanted. I know we are not relationship counselors, but guess what! If you see that a couple has totally different agendas you want to at least to make the effort to help them get in unison. If you don't, you may get something like what happened with another couple: The husband made the decision and signed the contract, and when he asked his wife to sign she made sure that everyone there knew she was doing it only because he asked her to. Believe me, that is not an experience you want to have.

Communication is huge, and you need to become a master when you work with international customers. Communication is also an ongoing process, before, during and after—yes, AFTER. Of course, you want the customer to come back to you for more!

Customers can have a short memory, so make sure you communicate with them, even when they are not planning to buy or sell. One day they will, and you want to be there at the right time and the right moment.

Follow-up

Why Follow-up Is So Important:

Follow-up is the key to new business with the same customer. If someone buys from you, at some point they will need to sell and usually buy again. What if you make the effort to maintain that customer, even though they may sell five years from now?

Follow-up is critical with first-time international customers because they do not know the process, even though you explained it to them, because they haven't experienced it yet. They forget about things or don't think they're as important as you know they are. For example, a customer from Venezuela did not want to include the property taxes in the mortgage. He made the commitment that he would pay it himself every year. We need to be on top of him every year and this has been a challenge. At one point he almost lost the condominium because even though we reminded him, he went on a trip and didn't pay until he got the notice that he was losing the property.

Working with international customers requires, in some cases, babysitting and hand-holding. You want to make sure that they are following the rules of the game (taxes, mortgages, insurance, etc.). Remember, they are not in the US, so keeping them posted about anything that could affect their property is the smart thing to do. The best way to keep all your customers up to date is a monthly newsletter that reaches not only your customers but other potential customers.

Follow-up before and at Closing:

Know the efficiency of the postal service in your target country. Will your customers receive the communications about the closing on time? If not, find other ways to communicate with them, and let the title company know these alternatives too. At the same time, it is very important to follow up with the title company on what they need from your customers. Be on top of every step of the closing process, with the customer and with the title company.

Before closing, if they are looking to be approved by the bank, contact the person at the bank about the approval status. And if they won't be able to travel for the closing, they will need to close at the embassy in their country. Go over the process with them, the title company and the bank so everyone is on the same page. If they are buying new construction, most of the buildings come without flooring or paint. Make sure they understand that. You may have to give them the names of two or three flooring and paint companies to get that completed before the condo or house goes up for rent, or they want to use it. One of the most common complaints I hear from international customers when I do my events is that they did not know that the flooring was not included. What happens is that the Real Estate Agent says that the property comes "decorator ready" and assumes the customer understands what that means. It could be a great idea to have a list of terminology to give to your customers at the first meeting. Even better, you could have it online so they have a written resource 24/7.

Follow-up on the Rentals:

This one is VERY important. I had a customer who, three months after we rented his apartment, told me that he had never received any payment from the tenant. I put my customer in touch with a lawyer to contact the tenant and either get the money or start the process of eviction. After that experience, I began following up with my international rental customers every two months to see how they are doing with their tenants.

You also want to ask them if they are paying the association dues. In one experience the association changed companies and needed the owner to sign another approval for a direct deposit to the association's new account. Usually the new association sends out letters via the regular postal service, but depending on how reliable the postal service is where your customer lives, he/she may or may not receive it. In this particular case, my customer never received that letter. The months passed until he got a collection letter from a lawyer via a courier service. It said that he had to pay the monthly payments he owed, plus interest, plus the lawyer's fee, all within thirty days. We negotiated after they understood that the customer never received any notification about the change of association.

Your customer needs to check every month that the maintenance and/or association dues are being deducted from their bank account. If they are not, they need to contact the association immediately. Usually the customer will call you and ask you to support them in doing that.

Another common situation is when the tenant leaves and the owner asks you to rent it again. They will need your support to get the property painted and cleaned, and maybe more. Have people on your team who can take care of that.

Services that Make the Difference

Customers would like to work with you for a variety of reasons, but what makes them stay with you are the services you offer that are different from everyone else's.

Think out of the Box:

Start brainstorming with your team about what your customer does from the time they decide to travel to your town until they go back. Are they traveling with kids? With pets? Are they combining business travel with pleasure? Do they know the city already? What do they like to do in their free time? What are their hobbies? If your customer loves tennis or golf and you have an important tournament in town, you can either get tickets for them or offer the service of getting the tickets. I am not saying that you have to pay for the tickets, but you can have your assistant get all the info about the price, dates, hours, and even make the call to buy the tickets over the phone. Keep in mind that you win when you offer your service before the customer asks for it.

Have a VIP Concierge Service:

You can either provide this service for them if you have an assistant, or hire someone to do it. You can also talk to your Broker and create a concierge department at your office that is available for all the international customers. Have links to websites, as well as phone numbers and addresses of what customers may need. If you do your research before the customer asks for it, you become a reliable resource. If I shared the things that customers have asked me to help them find, you would be impressed. I am not going over that now, but I will list the things that are the most common in my experience in the last few years.

Travel arrangements—Some customers are on vacation and would like to take tours, or make arrangements for further travel. You can help with confirmation of plane tickets, rental cars, etc.

Shows and events—Give the customer a list of what's going on in your city while they are visiting so they may go to the theater, movies, concerts, expos, etc.

Business Support—If the customer is planning to do business in the US they will need many services, but the most common I have been asked for are:

- *A local mailing address.* If the customer is buying the property as an investment, particularly a corporation, they will need a physical address in the US.

- *Virtual assistant.* Some of the customers, even though they live in another country, may have customers in the US so a virtual assistant who takes care of the messages is useful.

Additional services—As I mentioned before, think out of the box. You know your customer, so use a little bit of creativity and offer them unusual things, like:

- *Limo service.* Just make sure that your customer would appreciate this. Some people do not like it; some people love it.

- *Helicopter ride* over the area where they are interested in buying so they can take pictures and see what's going on in terms of new construction, empty lots, buildings, houses and commercial areas.

- *Boat tours. If the customer is buying on the beach or intracoastal waterway, take them for a ride in a boat so they can see a different perspective of the city.*

Create a "brick wall":

One of my early mentors told me that he was reading about the "brick wall" concept. He started drawing a brick wall and explained how each brick represents the services you offer your customers and how those bricks come together to form a wall that won't let the customer go away. I have to say that when he explained that concept to me, I understood then about "adding value" to your product or services. And to be honest with you I don't know from whom that "brick wall" concept came, but I do know it is one thing that made me see my job in a different way. It changed the way I was working. Keep in mind that the "brick wall" needs to be built on an ongoing basis and improved with time.

Think what your special service or services will be and how you are going to deliver to your customer in a way that will exceed their expectations, help them to achieve their goals, support them in the best way possible, and give them such a great experience that they will refer you to others and come back to you themselves.

Resources and Bonus Material

Instead of listing information here which will probably be outdated by the time you read this book, I invite you to visit www.ResourcesForInternationalRealEstateAgents.com for:

- Links to resource websites

- For available trainings and coaching programs

- Bonus chapters and updated content

- Hot tips

- News about the International Real Estate arena

- To network with other Real Estate Agents

- To subscribe to my newsletter

- Free conferences calls, and more

Also on the website, you can purchase and download a companion Workbook to *Success with International Customers*, which you can use to put into action what you've learned in this book.

Valeria Grunbaum is a seventeen-year sales and marketing veteran recognized for her exceptional ability to communicate with clarity, conviction, insight and dynamism on a full spectrum of topics about achieving success in the global marketplace. Long-standing clients and peers attest to her commitment to effect positive change in the hearts, minds and practices of organizations and individuals.

Valeria draws upon applied and successful business know-how that has secured her 'Top Producer' status in every industry she has endeavored. Also informing her messages are her personal life experiences and years of consulting with major national and international organizations ranging from international real estate brokerages to the American Chamber of Commerce, from global brands Procter & Gamble, Avon, DHL and Intercontinental Hotels to industry giants General Motors and Compaq. Her client roster reads like a veritable 'Who's Who' in corporate leadership.

Valeria is active with RAMB, the Realtor® Association of Greater Miami and the Beaches. She specializes in sales and marketing strategies, and working with international clientele. She has published articles on sales and marketing strategy and promotions, has served as a field expert for television, radio and print media, and has now written this book on selling to international clients. She has been the keynote speaker and lead presenter in numerous international conferences, has been invited to Latin America to train local and international sales agents, has taught and guest lectured at leading universities in Caracas, and has been recognized as one of the Top 50 Most Successful Women in Venezuela, by *The Daily Journal*.

Valeria is fully bilingual, in English and Spanish. She is an NLP practitioner and noted expert in sales and sales training. Her understanding of human nature, astute insights and vast experience in the Latin American market have made her one of today's most sought-after international realty strategists.

Website: www.ValeriaGrunbaum.com

Printed in the United States
127243LV00002B/1/P